Letter Tracing Practice!

Letter Tracing Book for Preschoolers

Copyright © 2018

All rights reserved. No part of this publication may be reproduced, stored in a retrieval system, or transmitted in any form or by any means, electronic, mechanical, photocopying, recording or otherwise, without the prior written permission of the publisher.

ISBN-13: 978-1986433310

ISBN-10: 1986433315

# Part 1 : Tracing Letter

Follow the dot lines to form the letters.

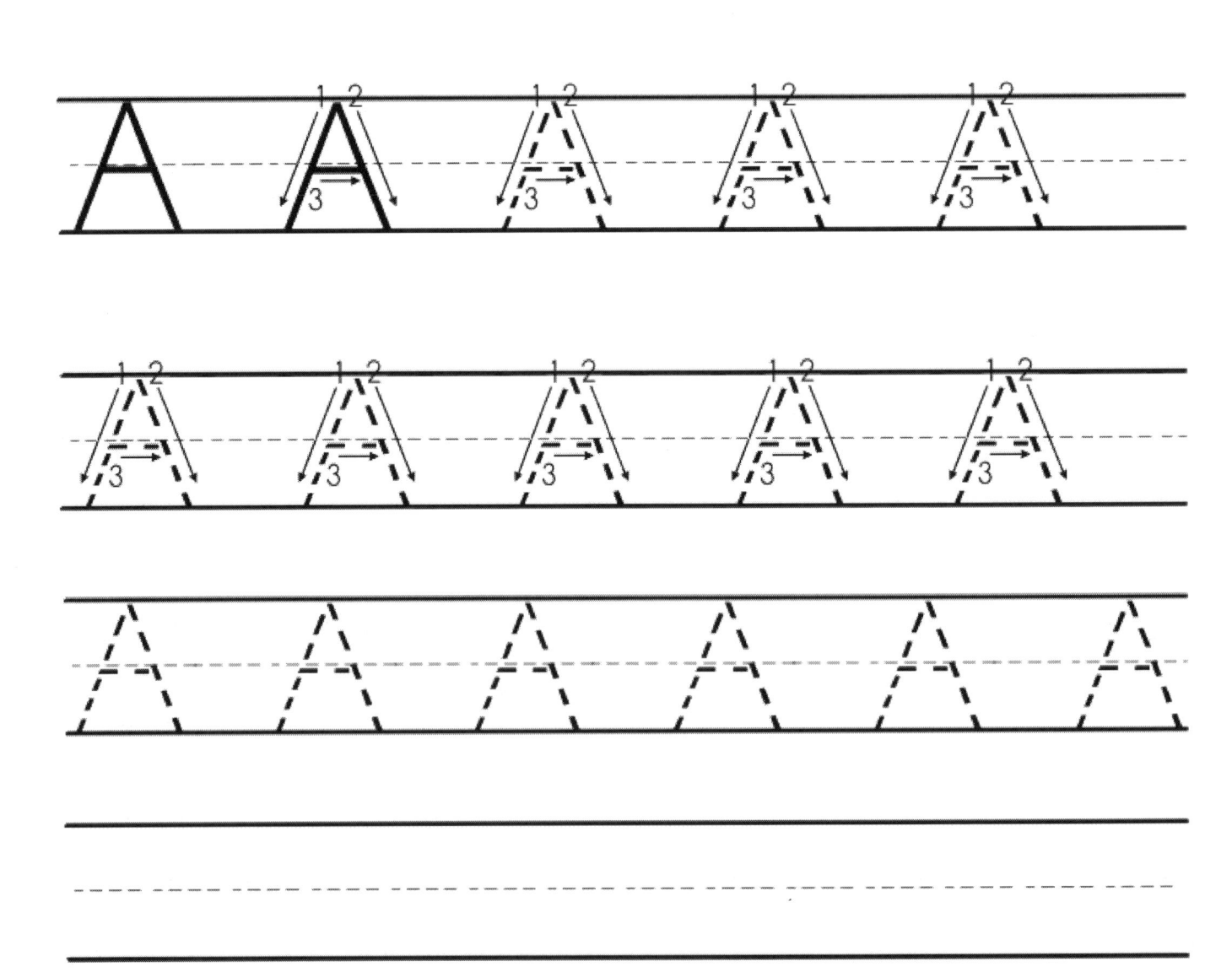

Ant

# Airplane

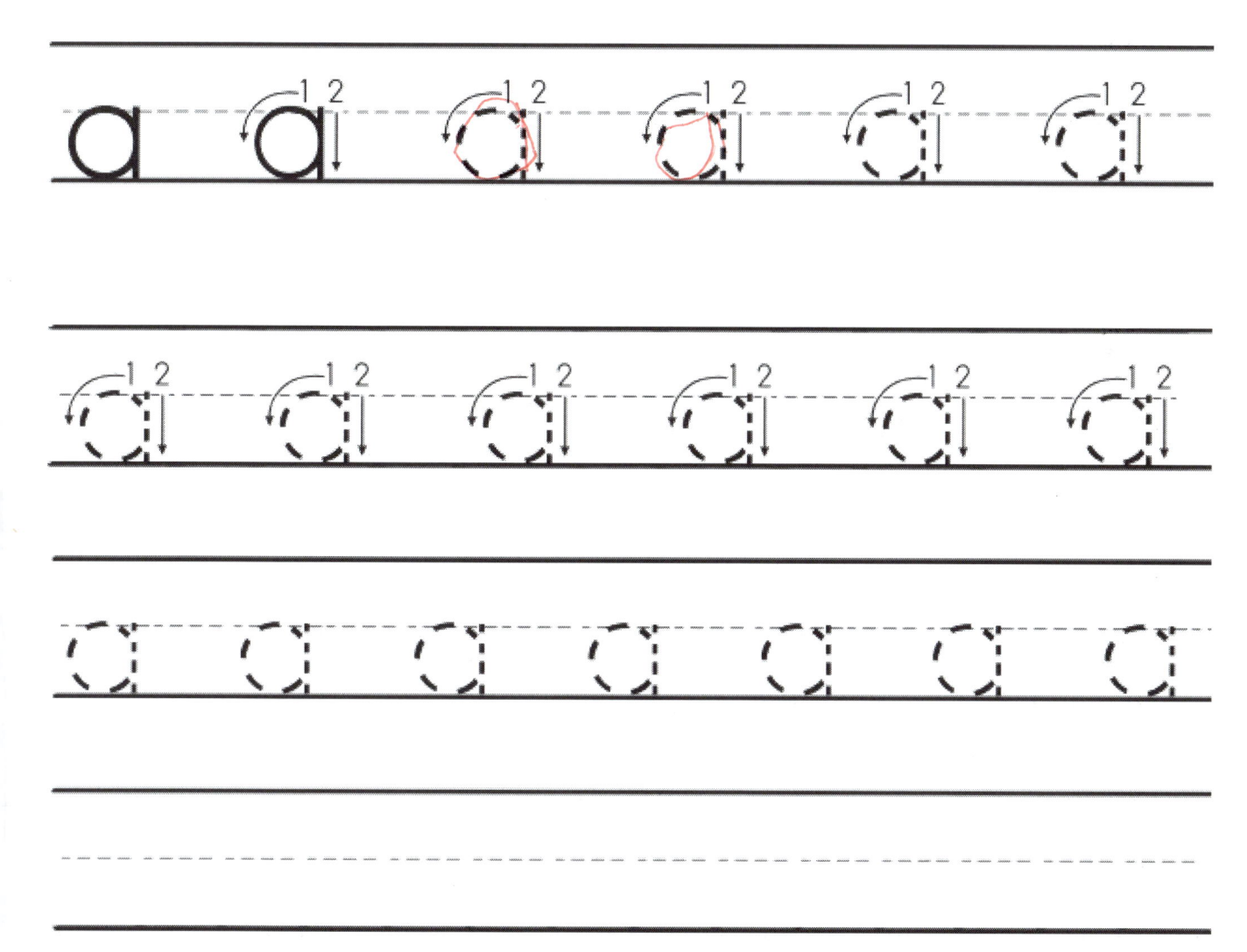

# Boat

# Bicycle

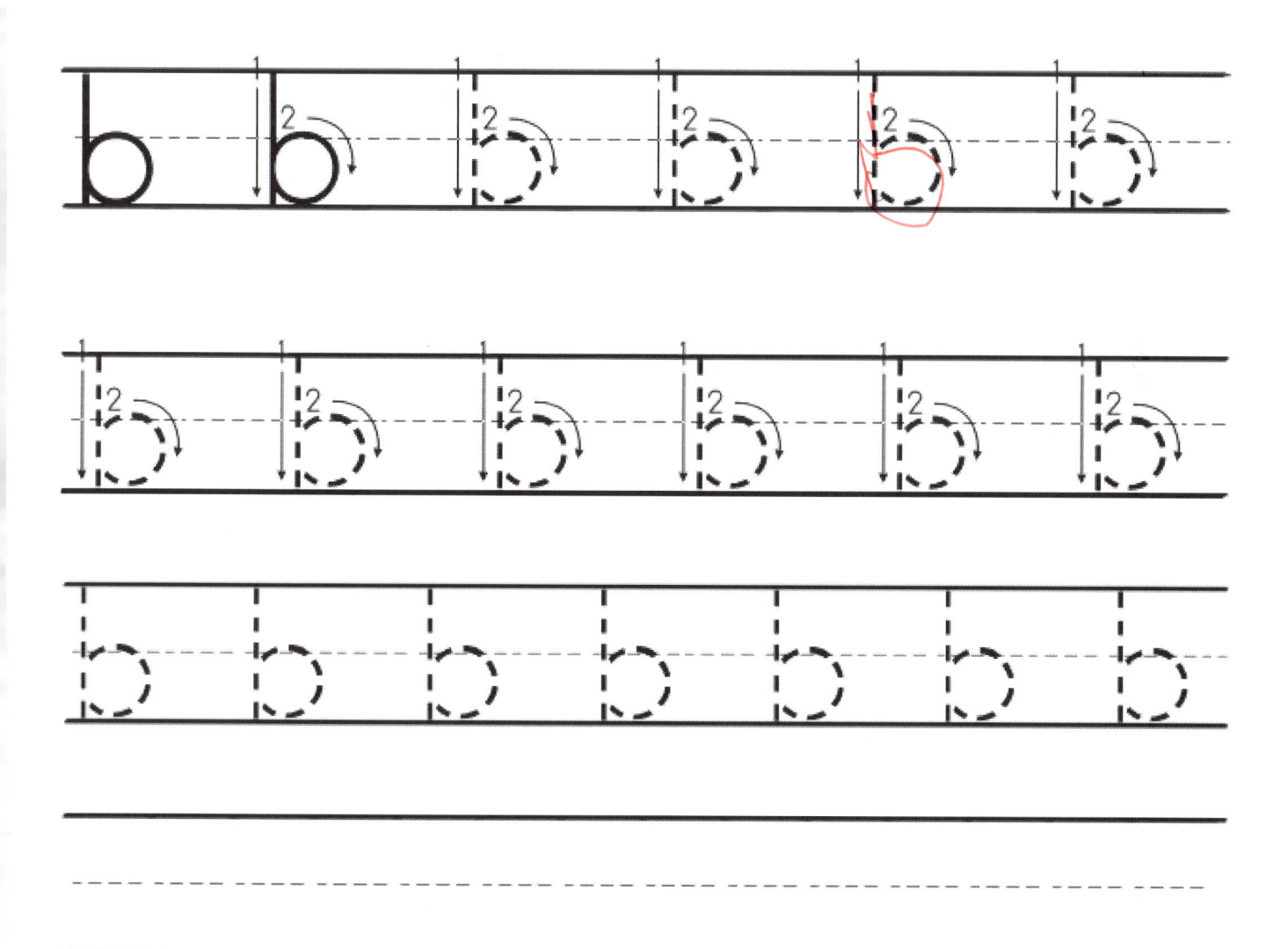

# Cow

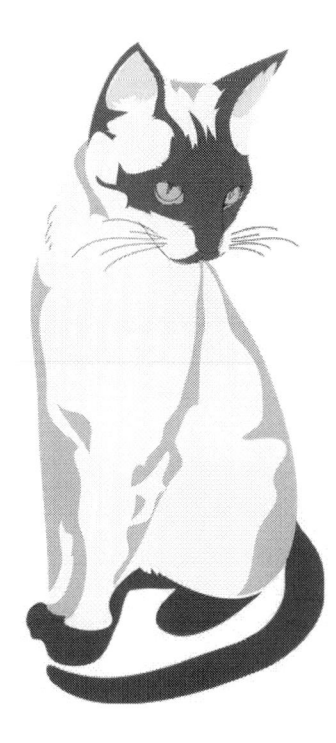

# Cat

# Dinosaur

D D D D D

D D D D D

D D D D D

# Dog

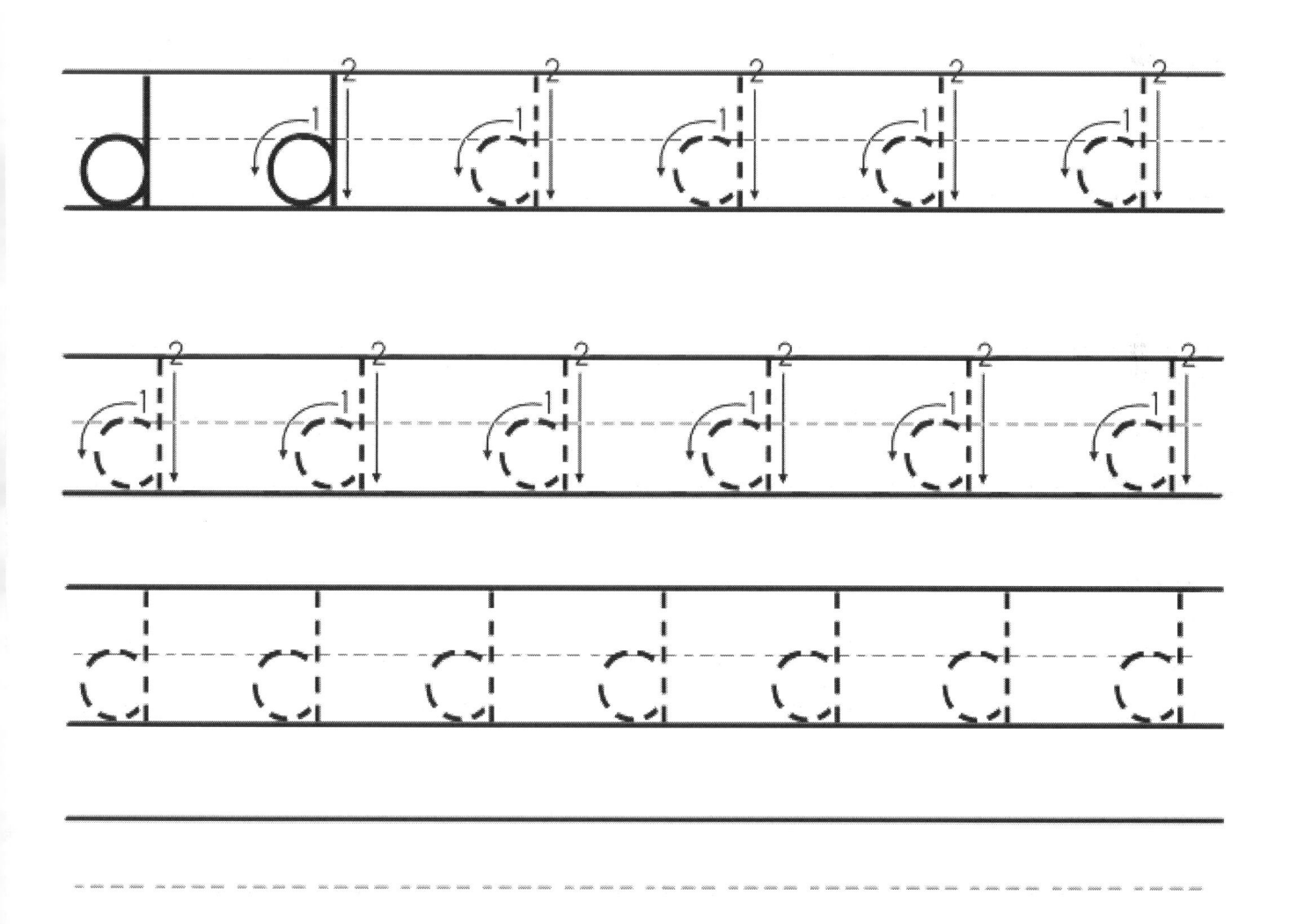

**Elephant**

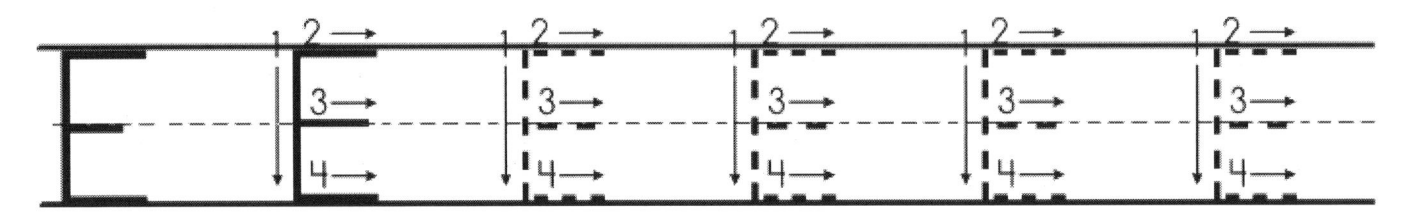

# Eagle

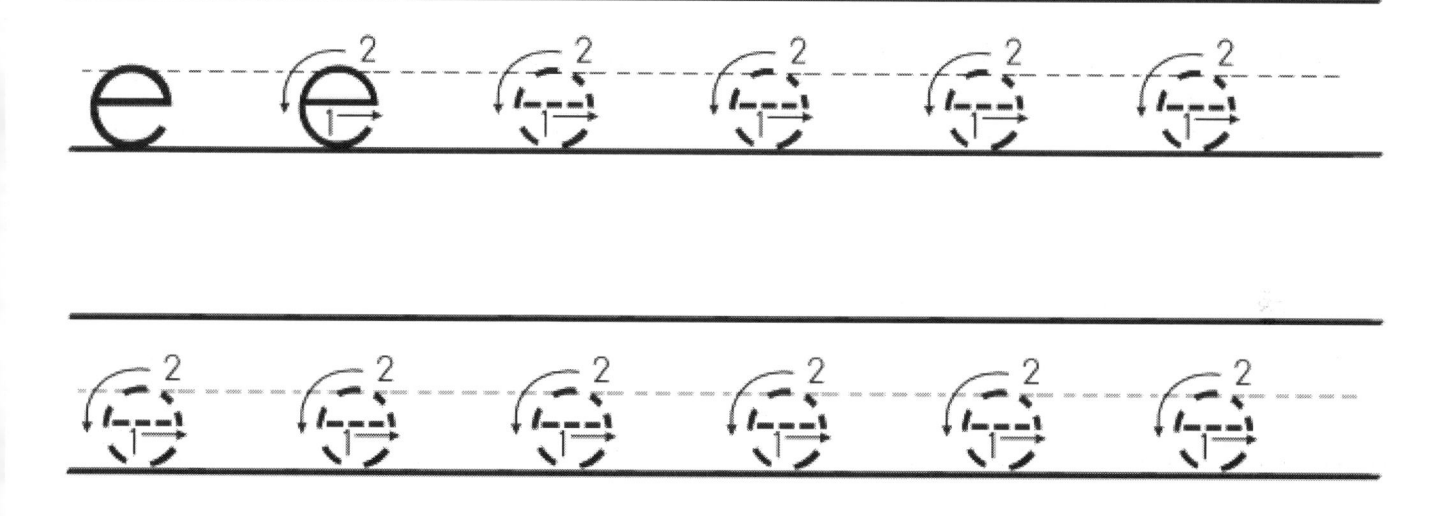

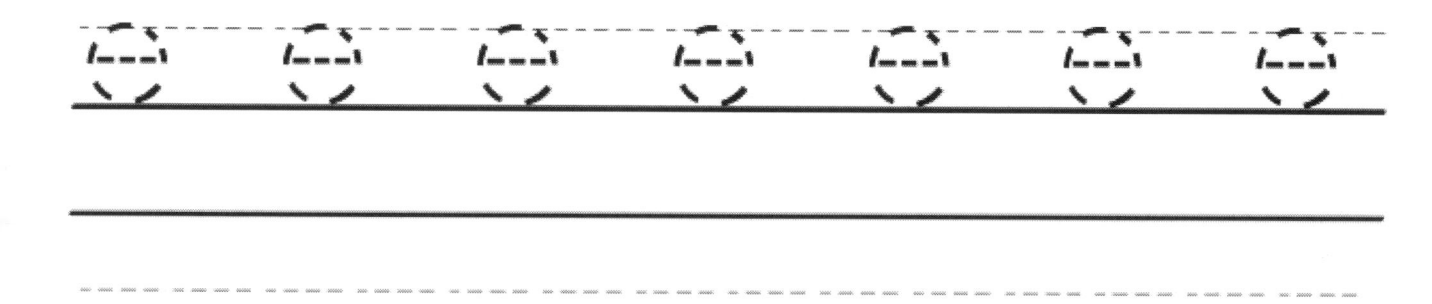

# Fox

# Flower

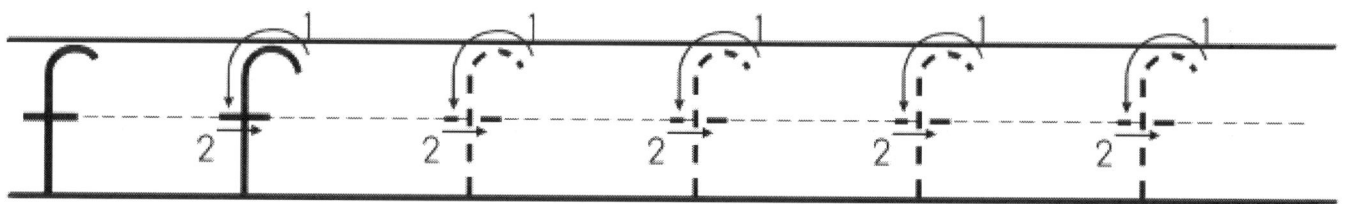

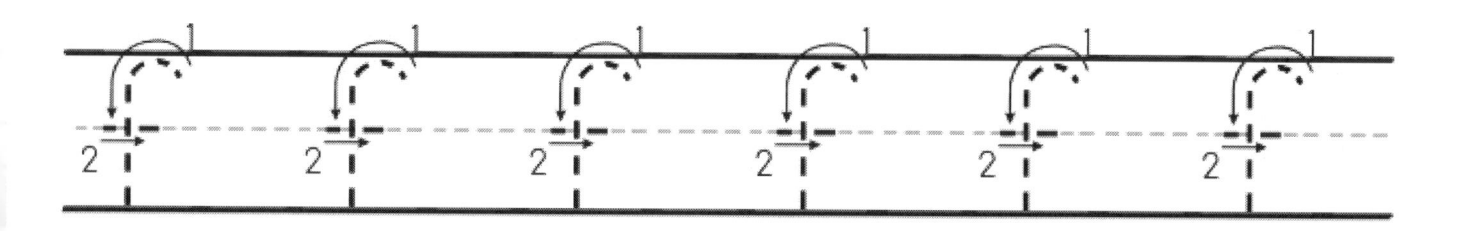

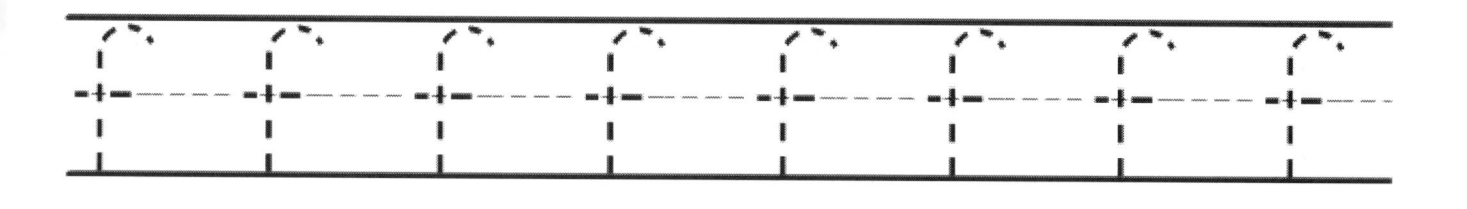

# Giraffe

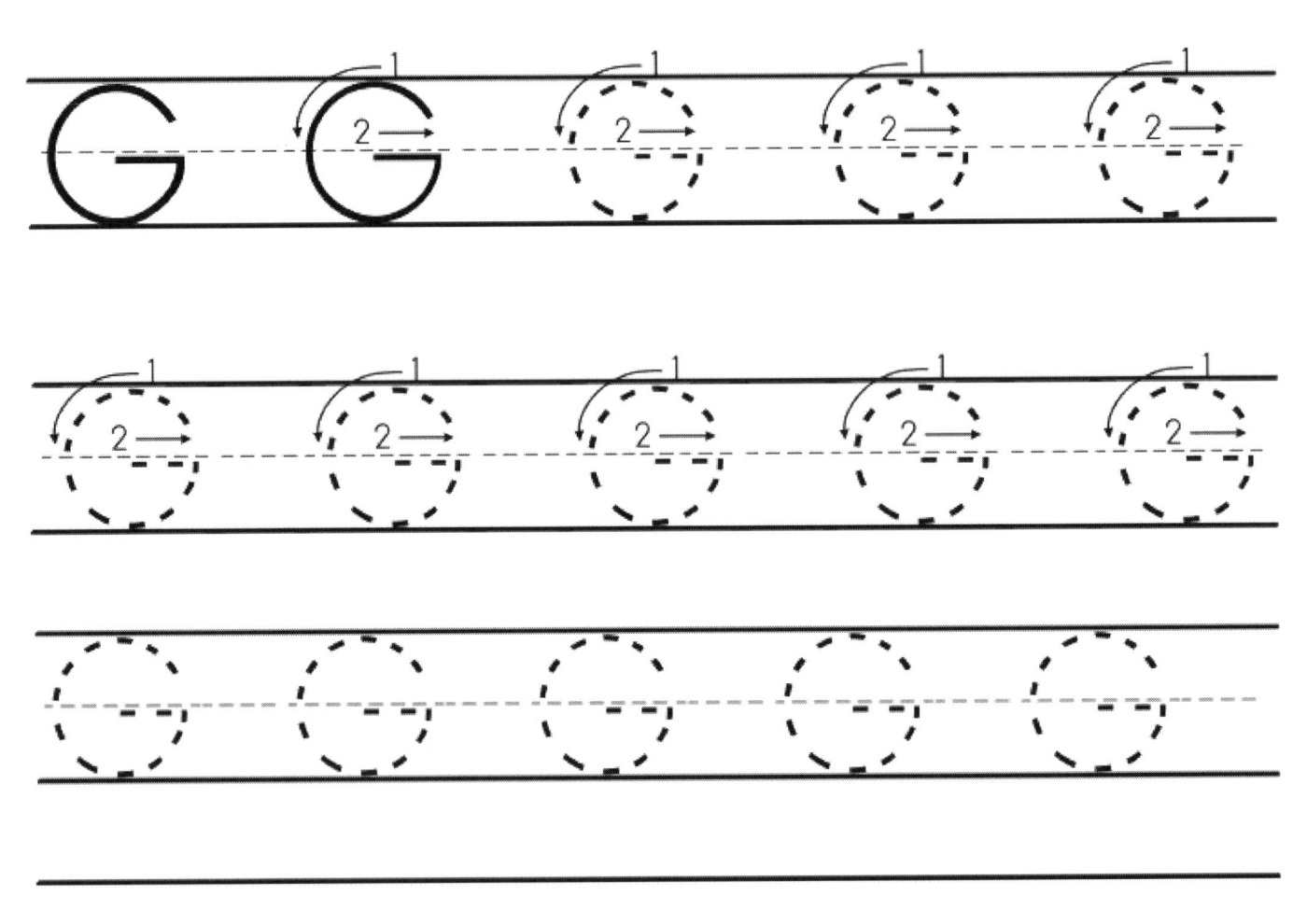

# Goose

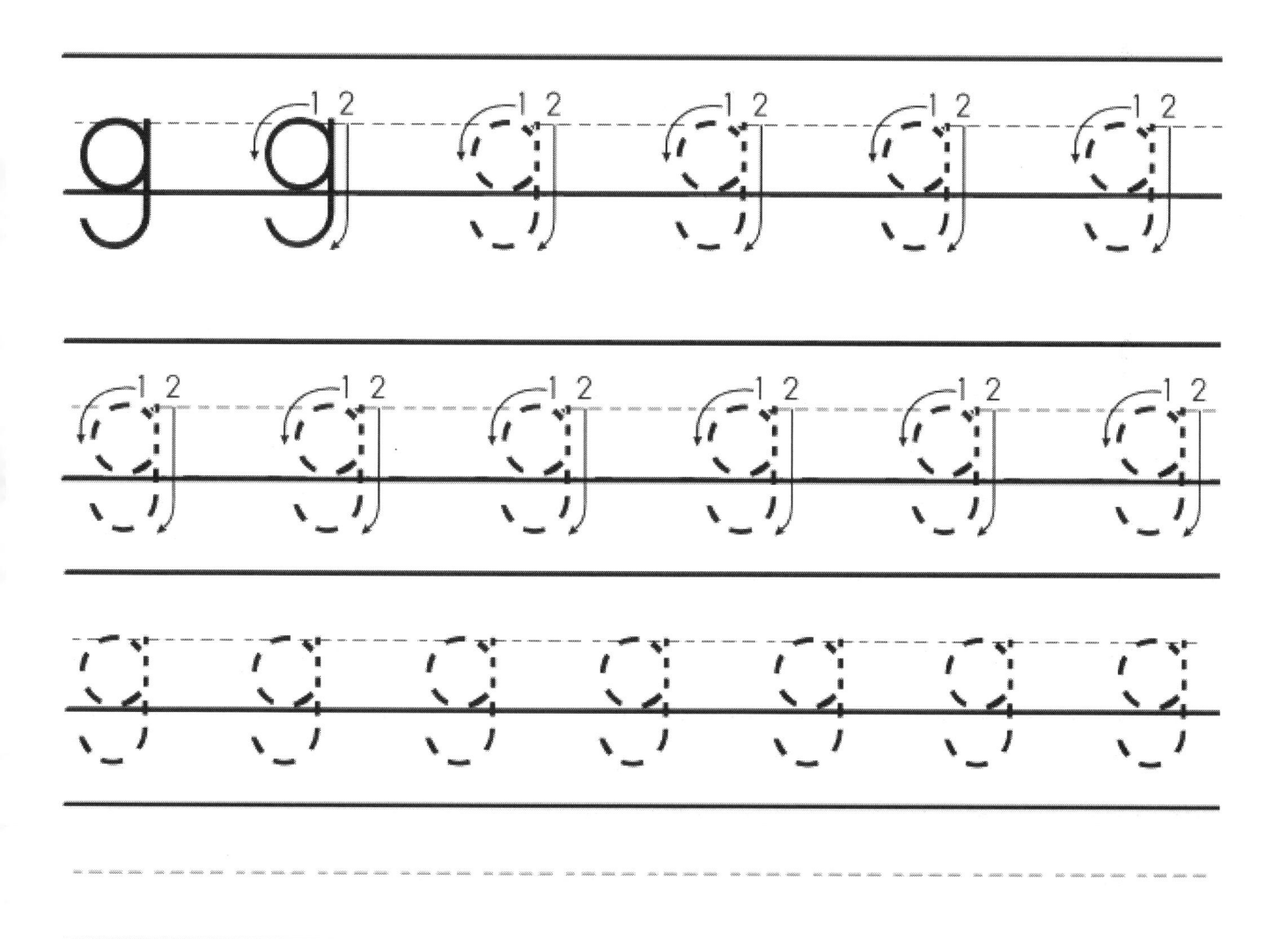

# Hippopotamus

# Horse

# I'm

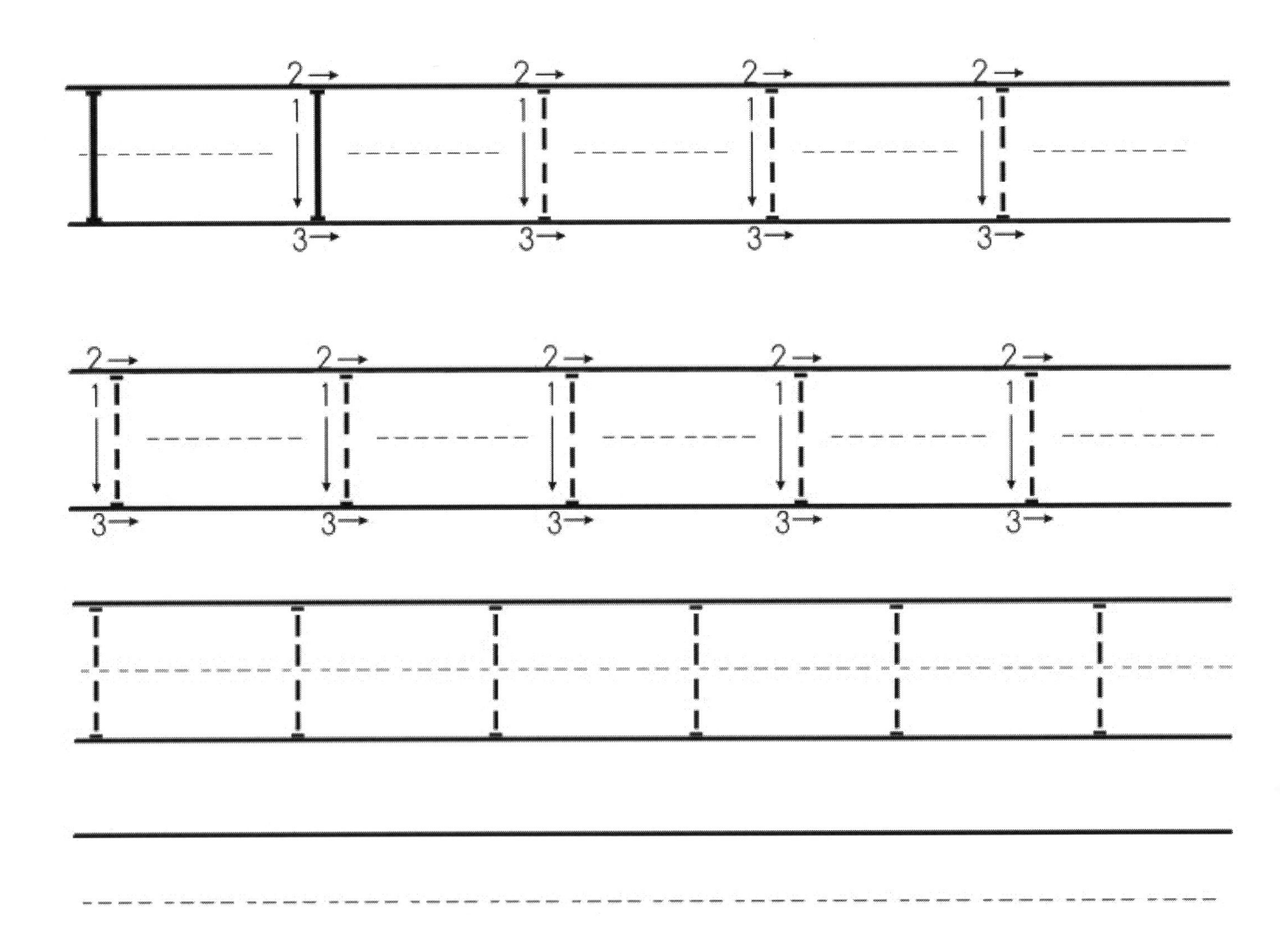

# Ice-cream

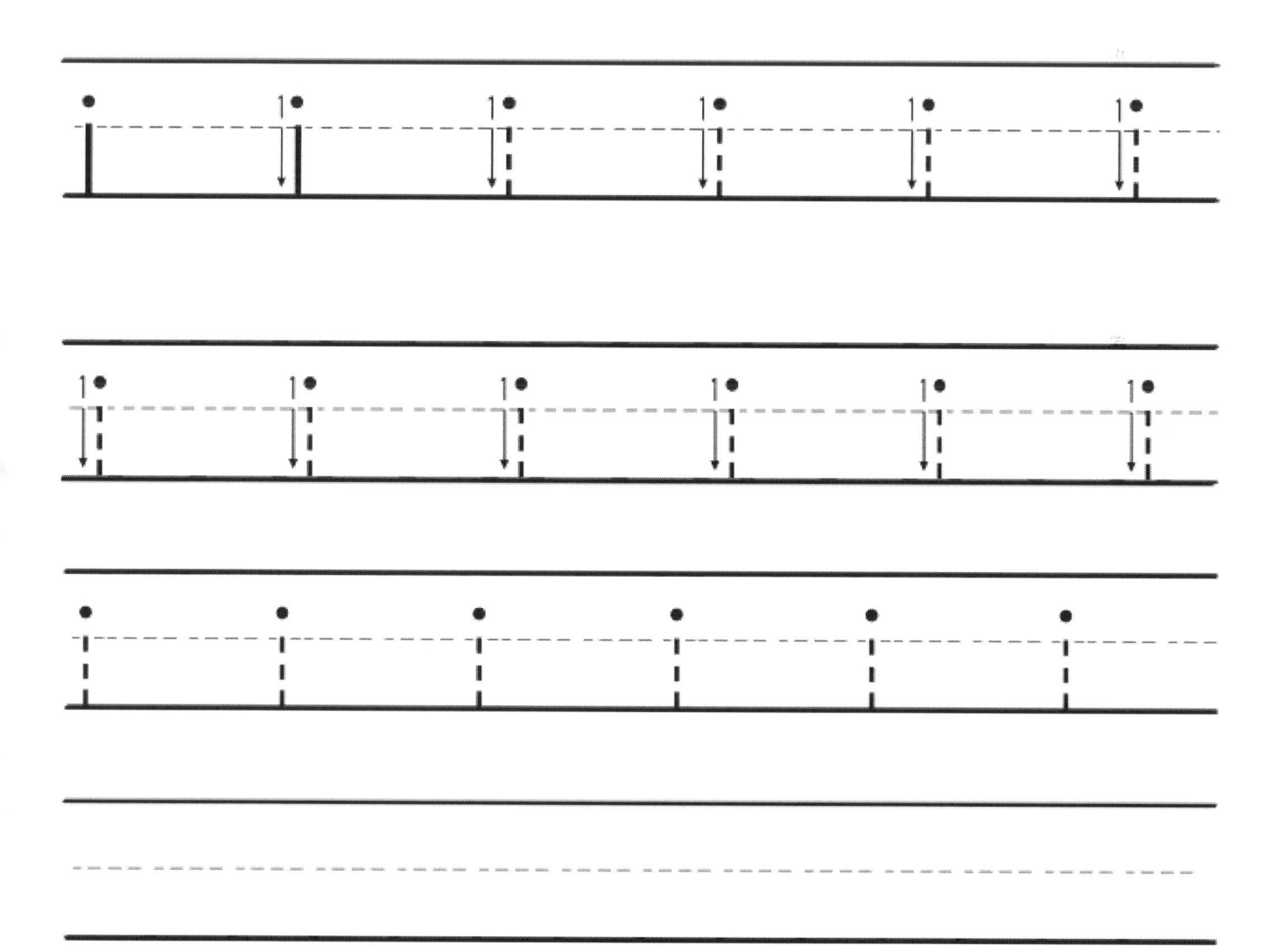

# Jacket

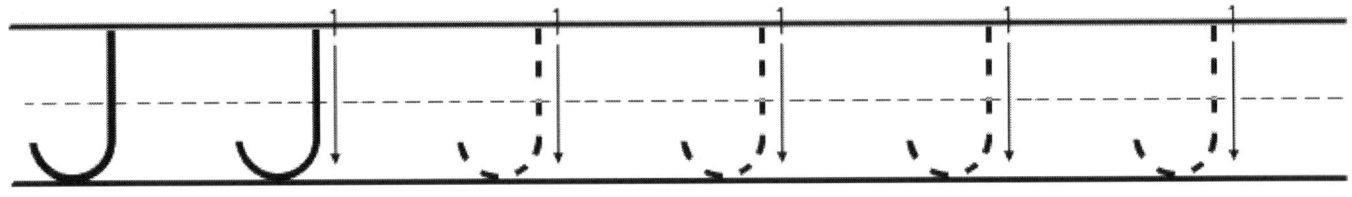

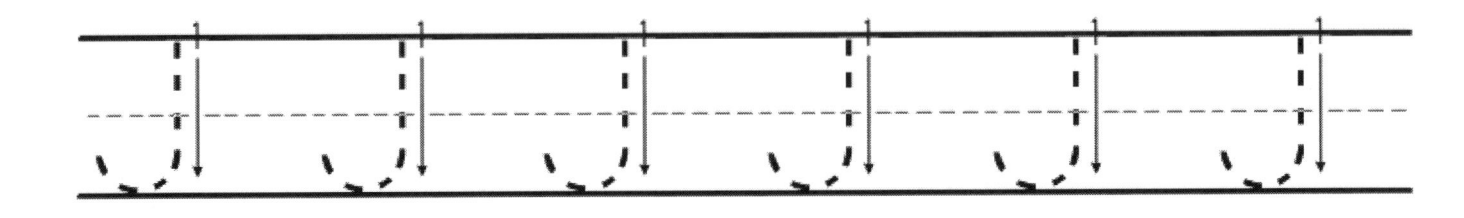

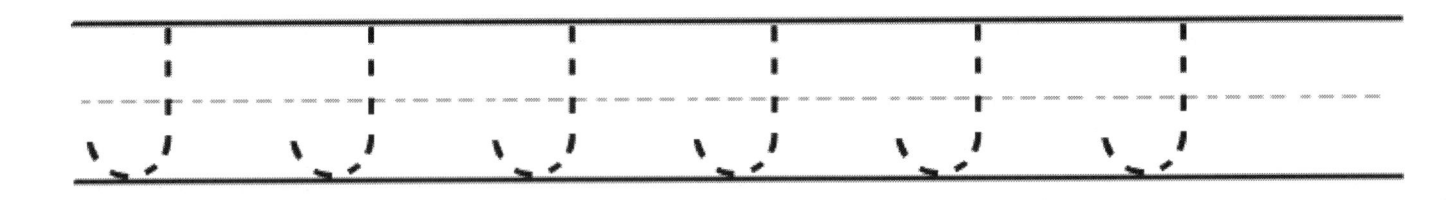

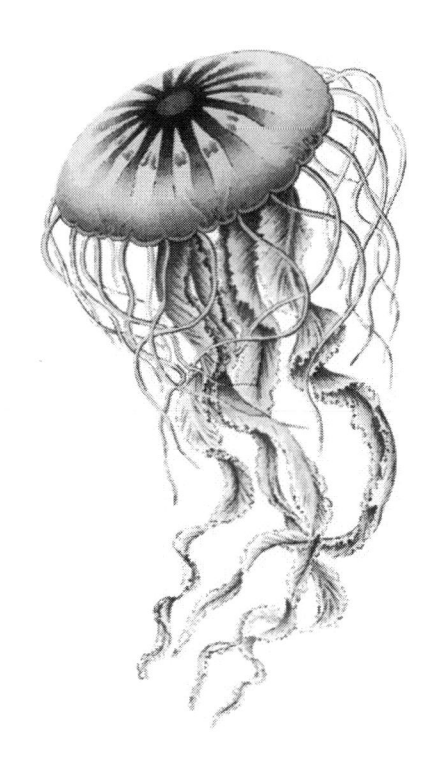

# Jellyfish

J J J J J

j j j j j

j j j j j

# Kangaroo

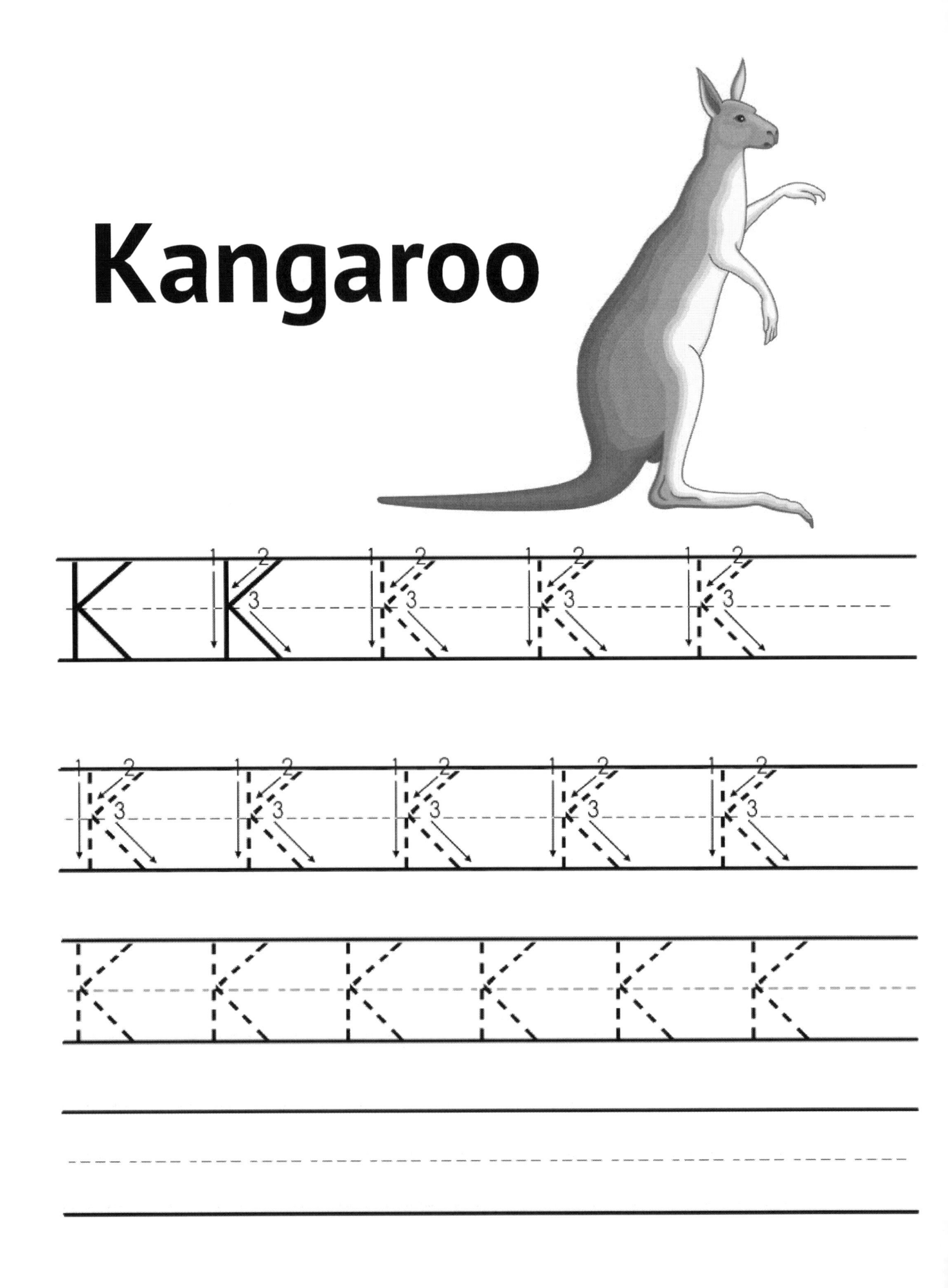

# Koala

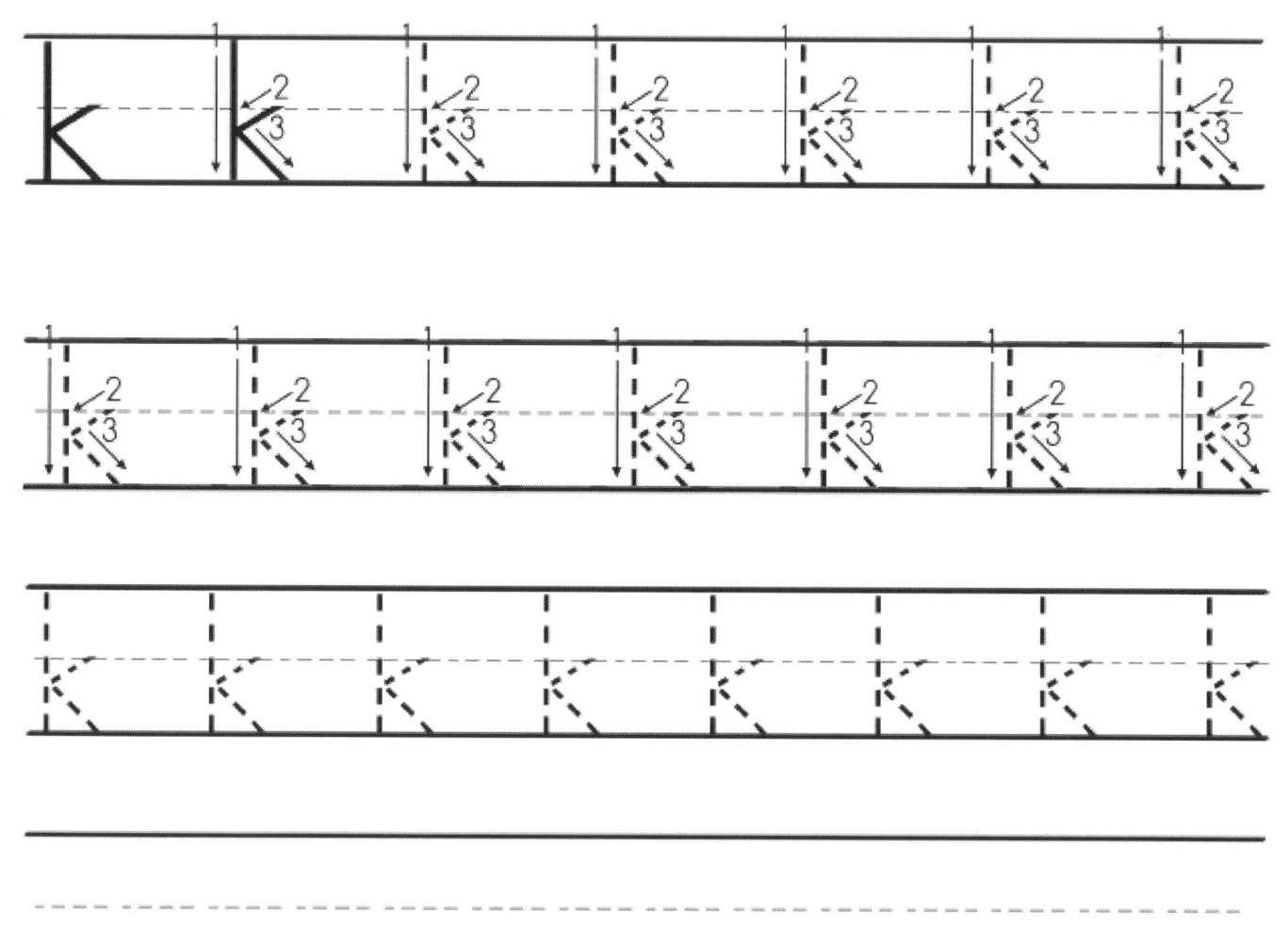

# Lion

# Llama

# Monkey

# Money

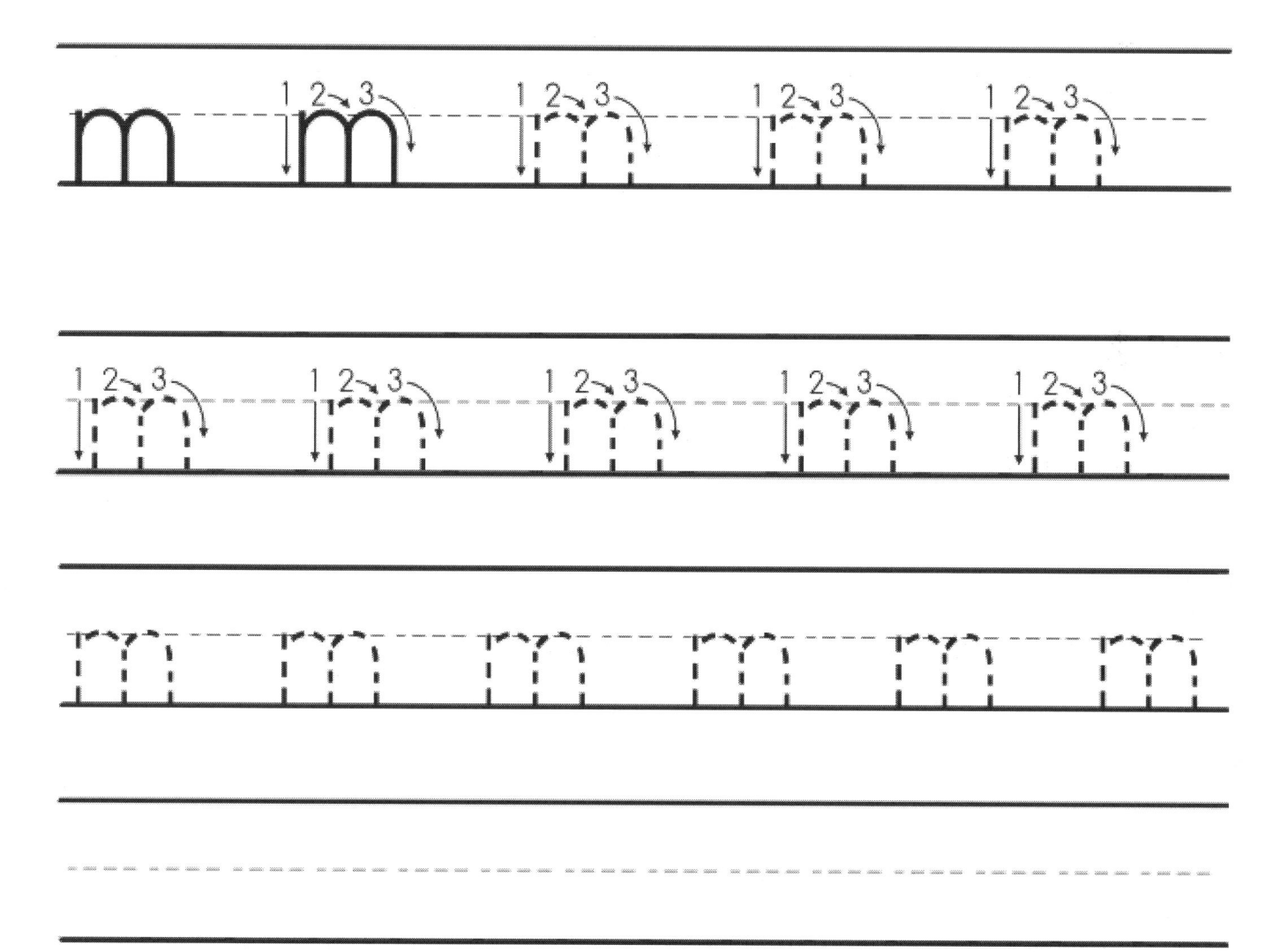

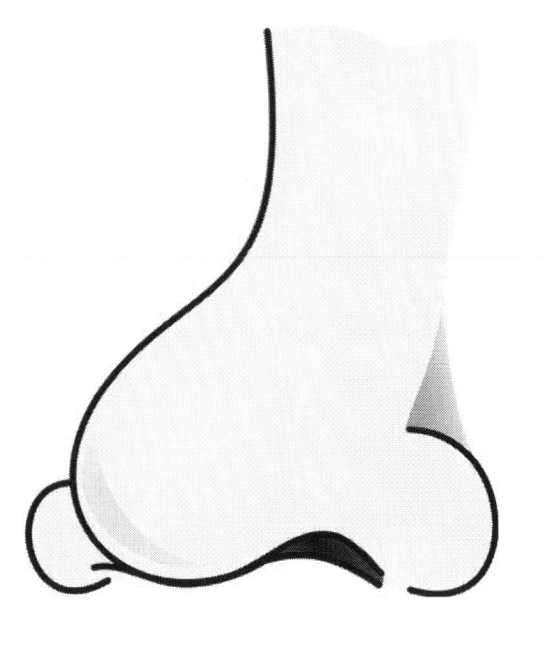

# Nose

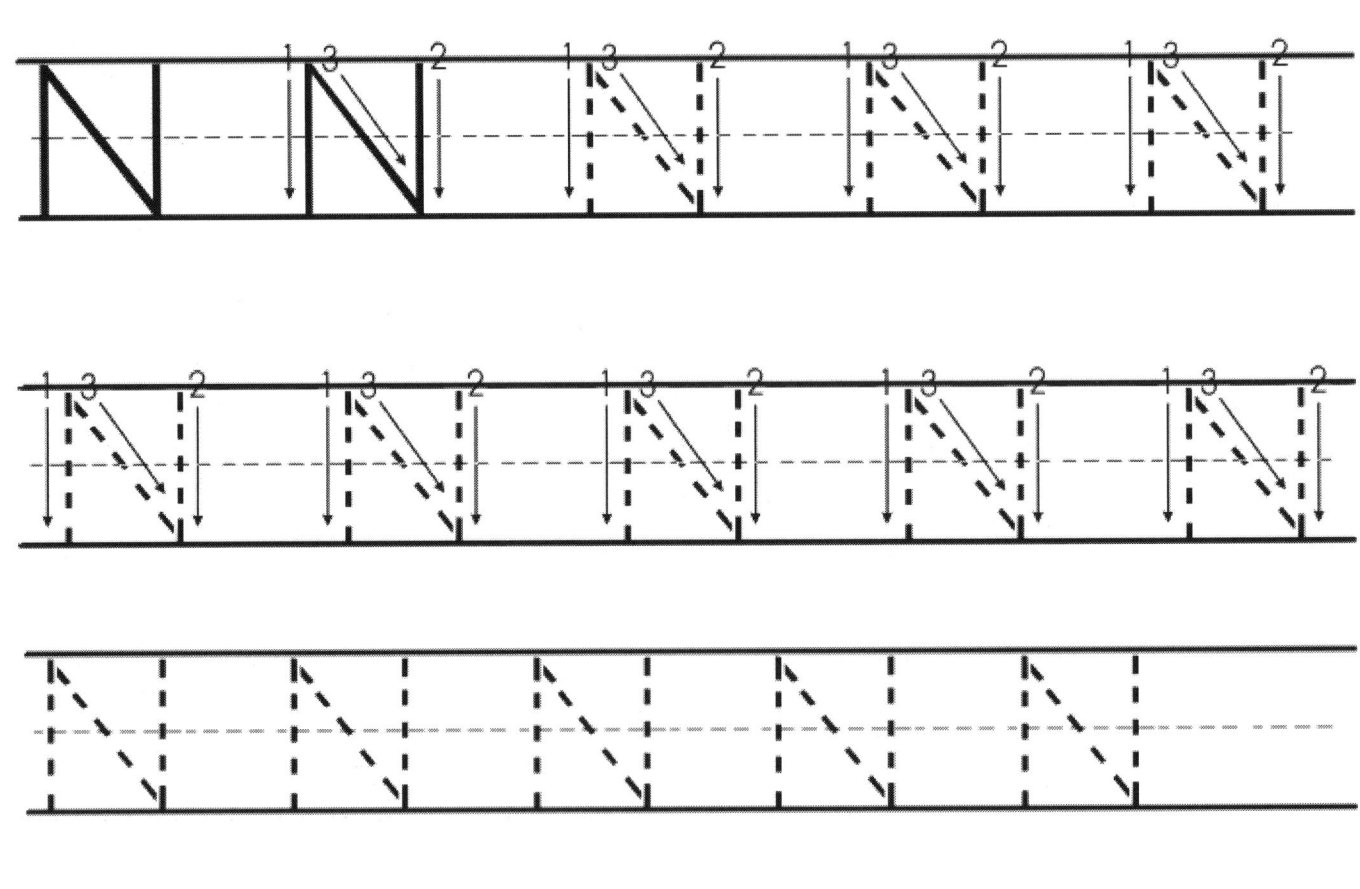

# Number

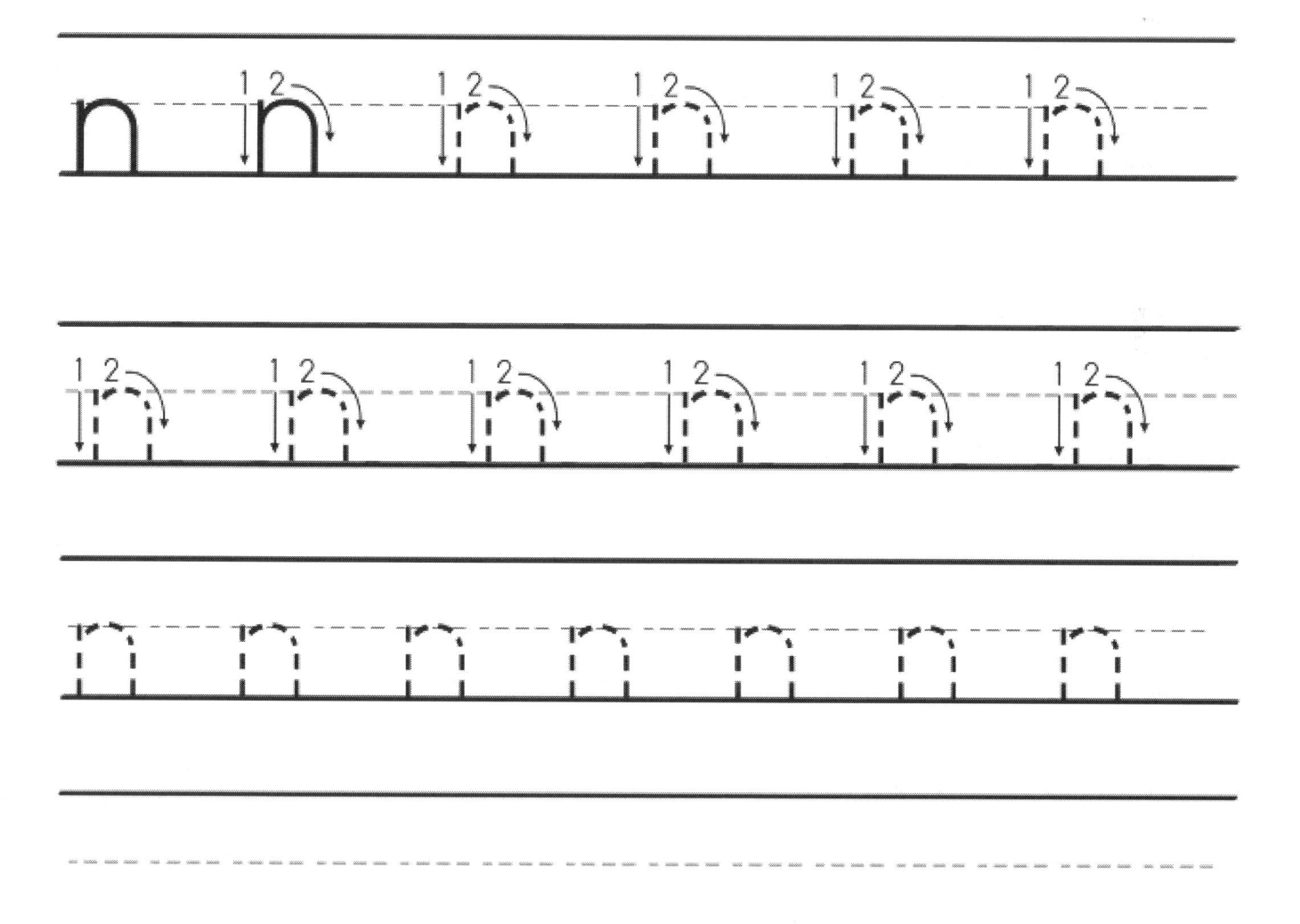

0 1 2 3 4
5 6 7 8 9

# Orange

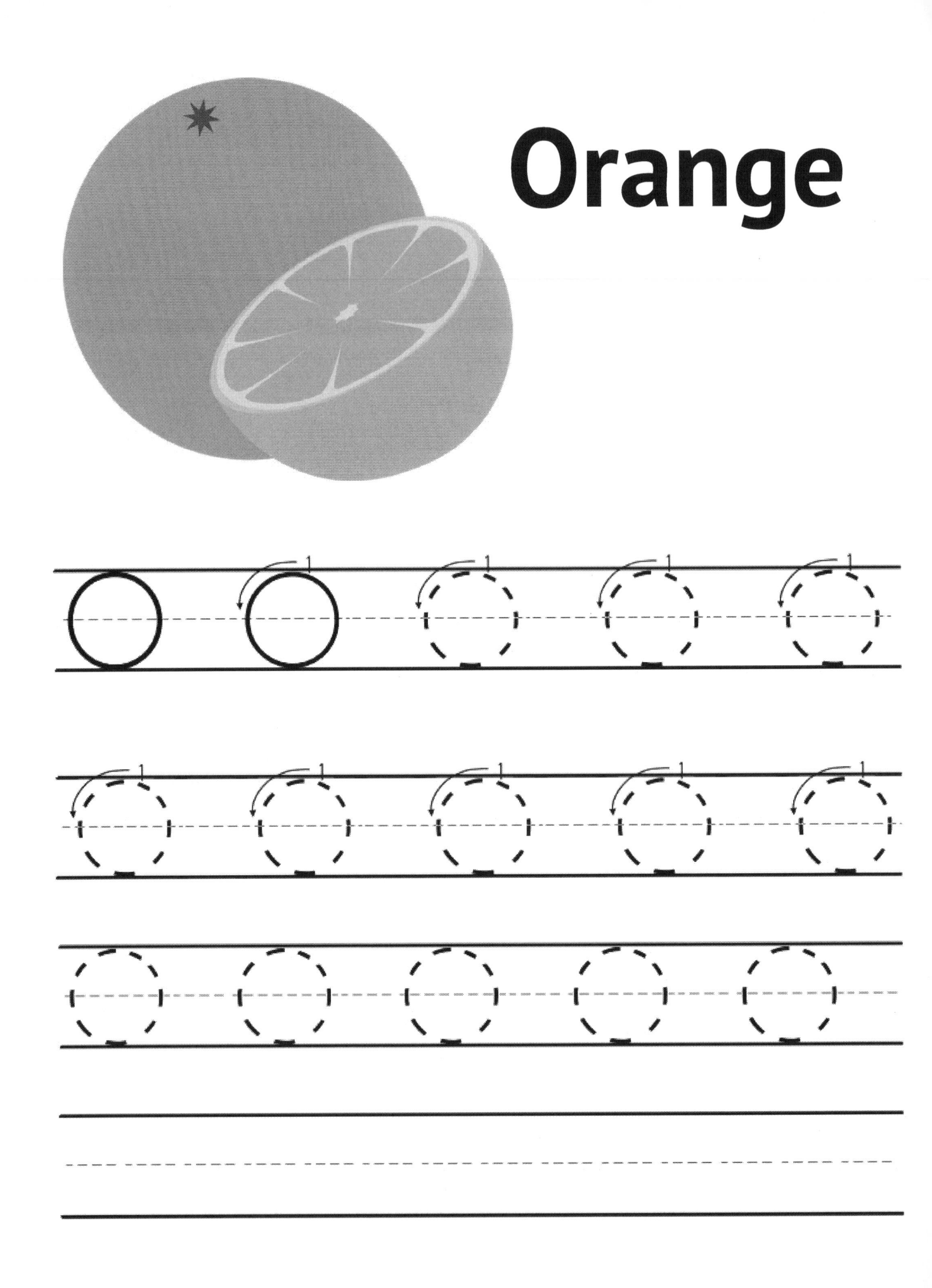

# Octopus

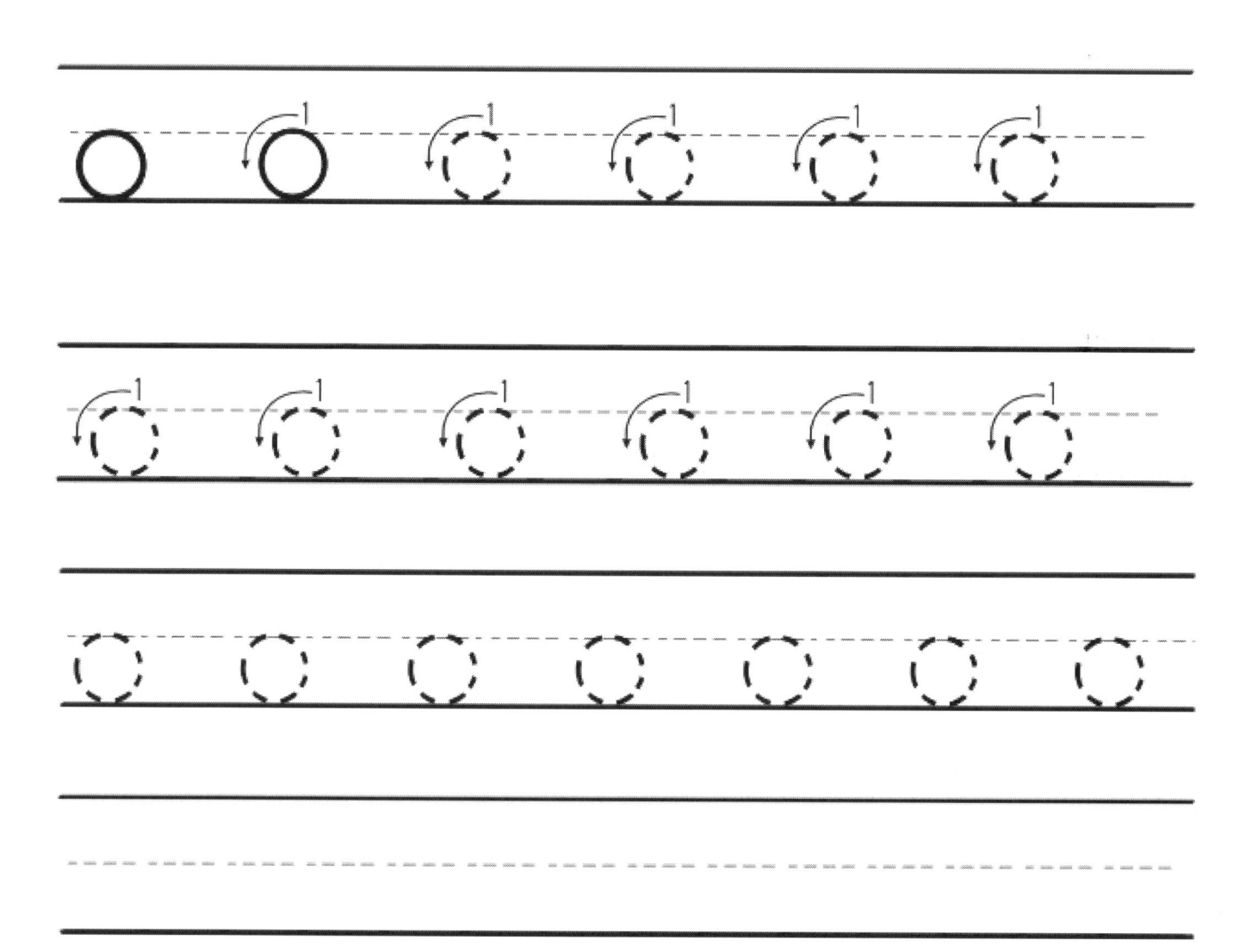

**Pineapple**

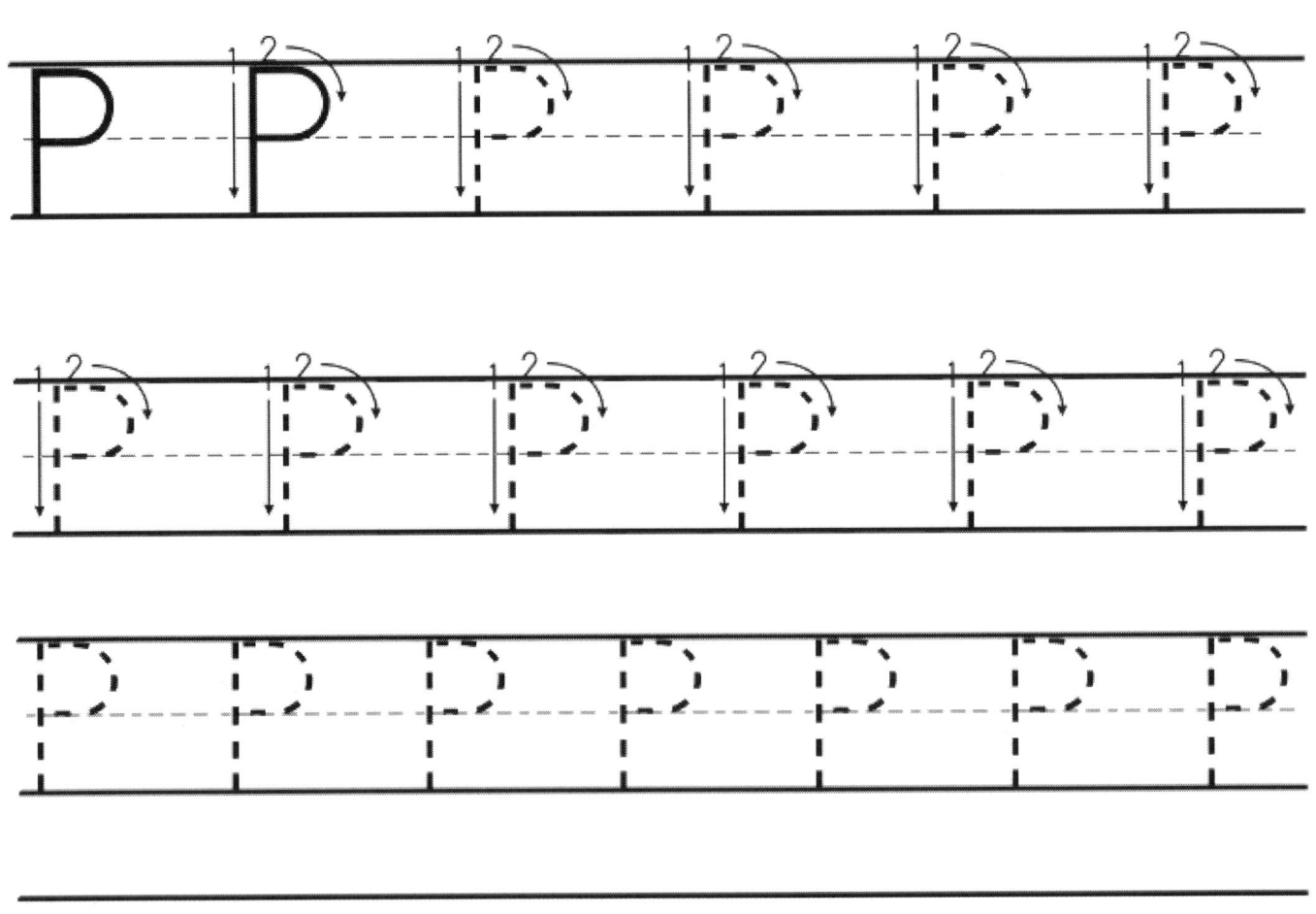

# Pirate

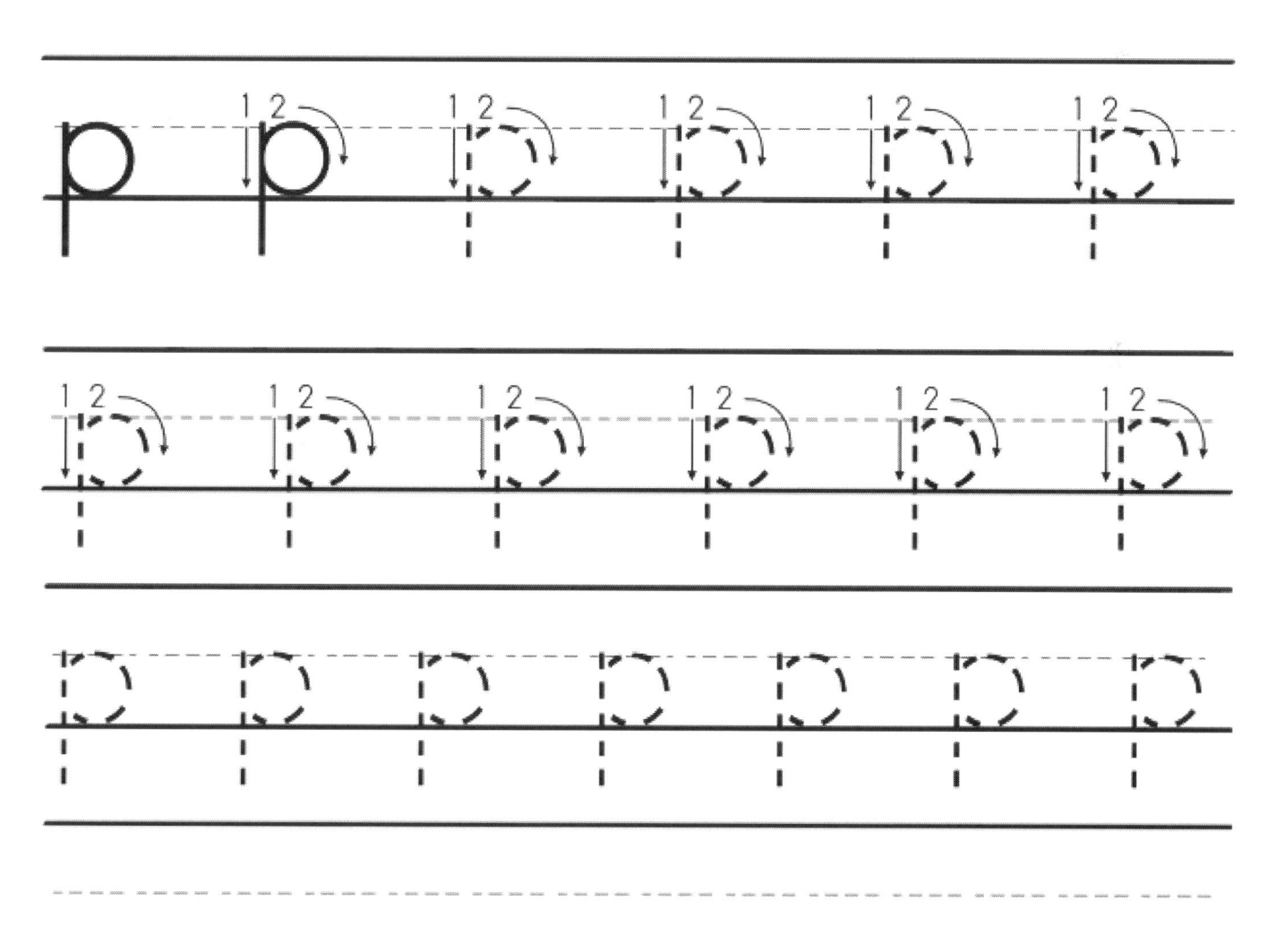

# Queen

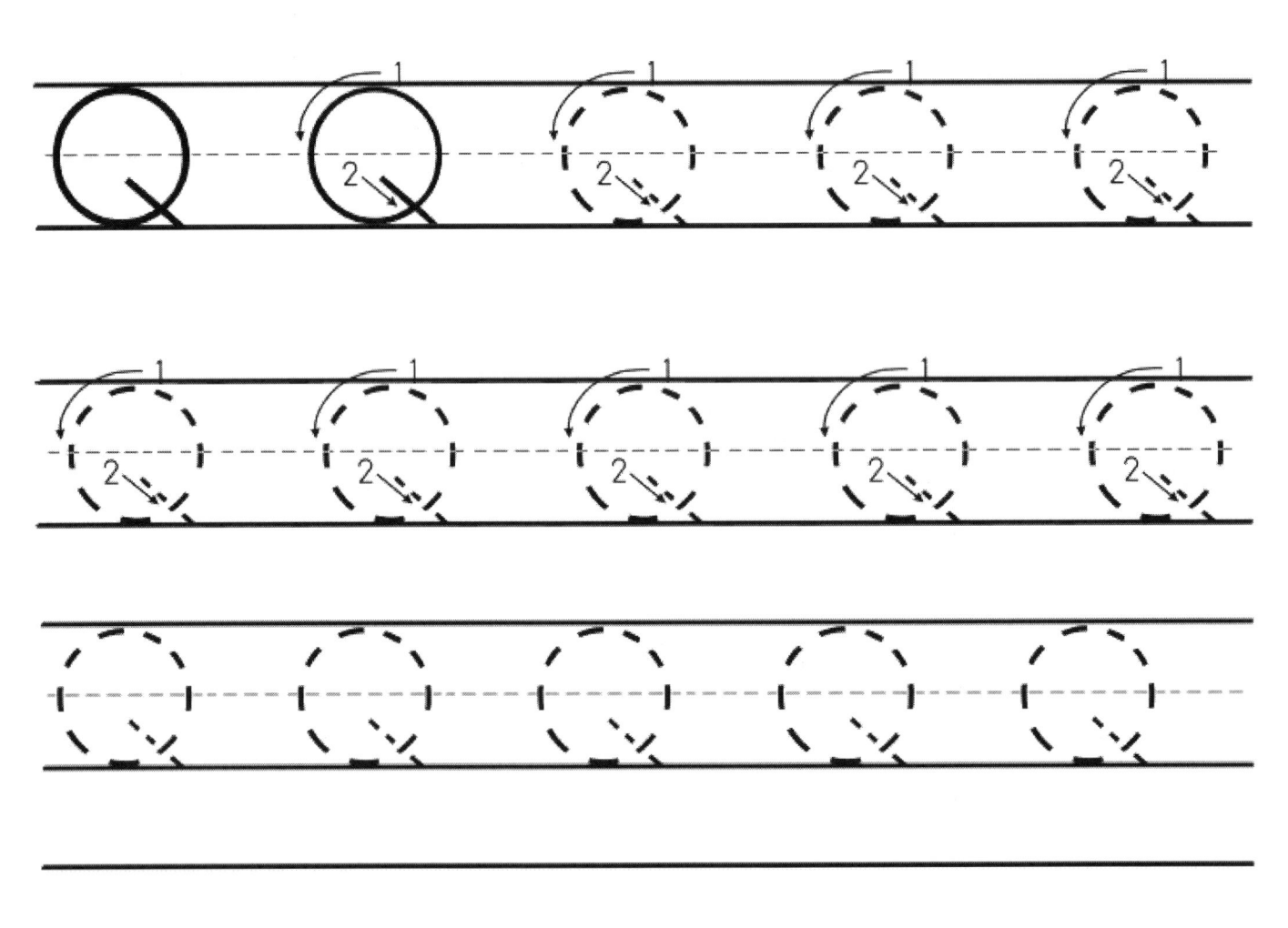

# ? Question

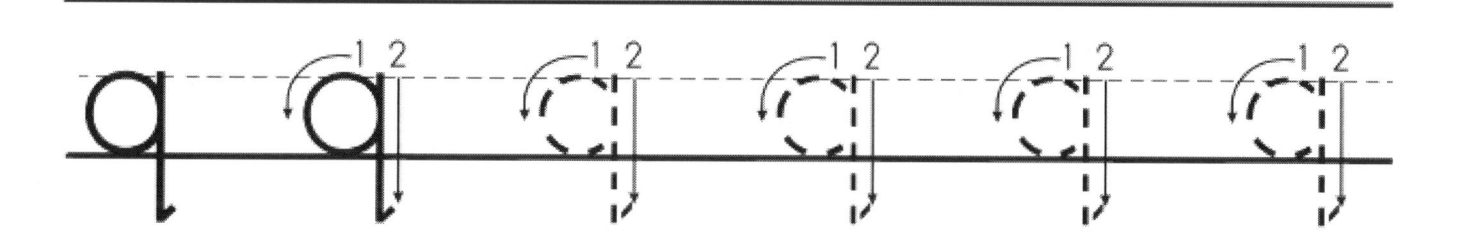

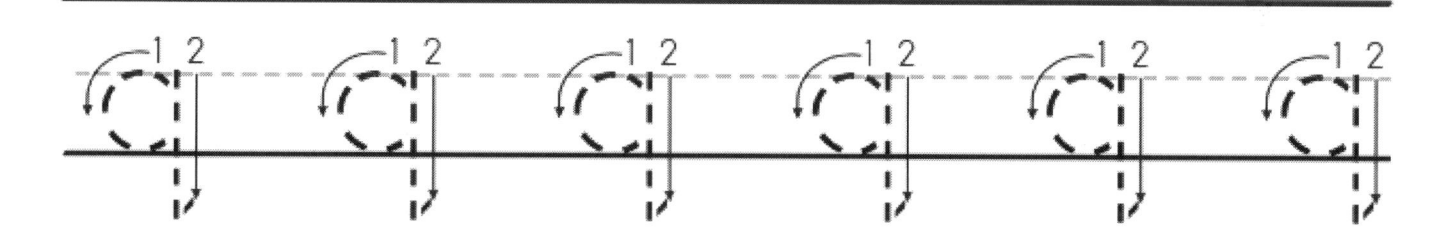

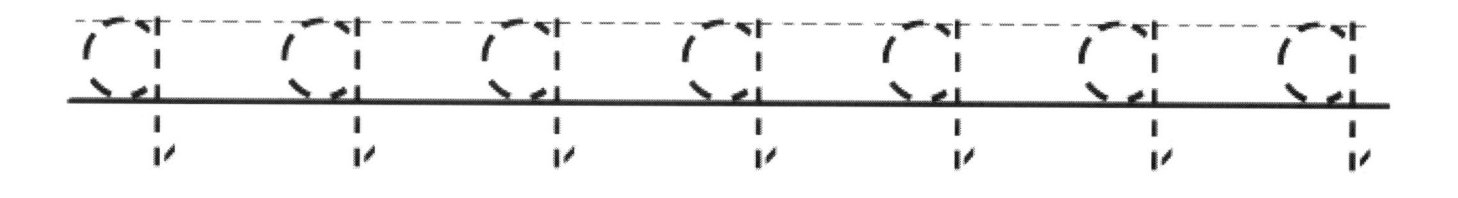

# Rainbow

# Rat

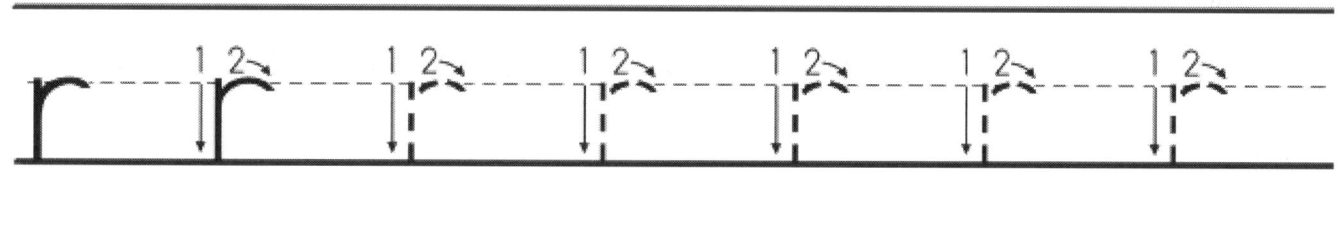

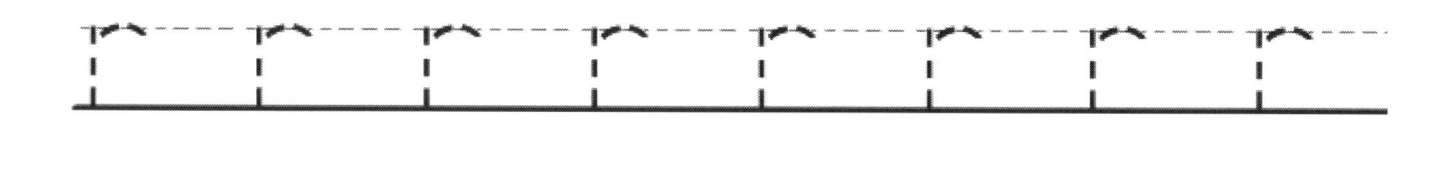

r r r r r r r r

r r r r r r r

# Snake

# Squirrel

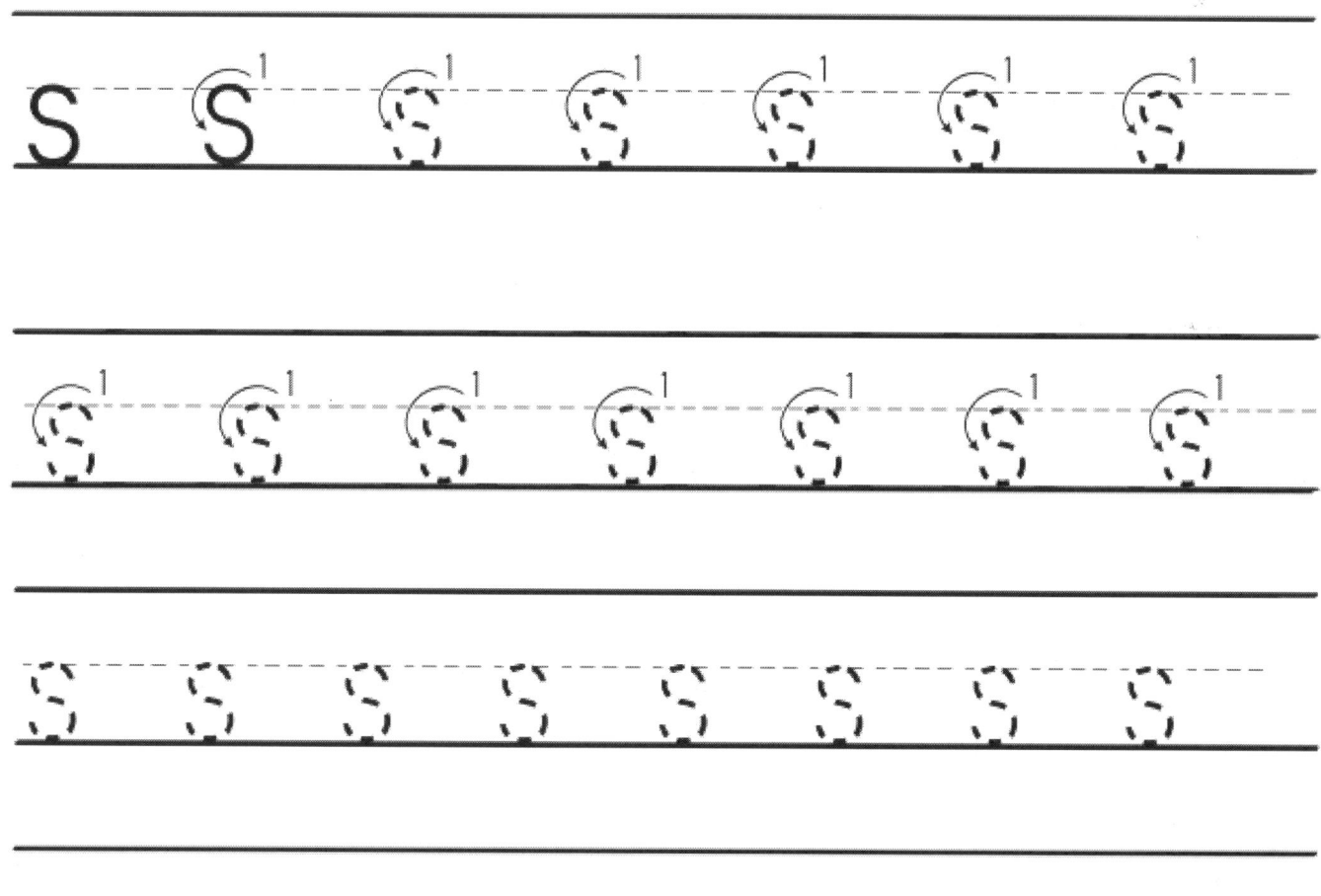

S S S S S S S S

s s s s s s s s

S S S S S S S S

# Tortoise

T T T T T T

T T T T T T T

# Tiger

# Umbrella

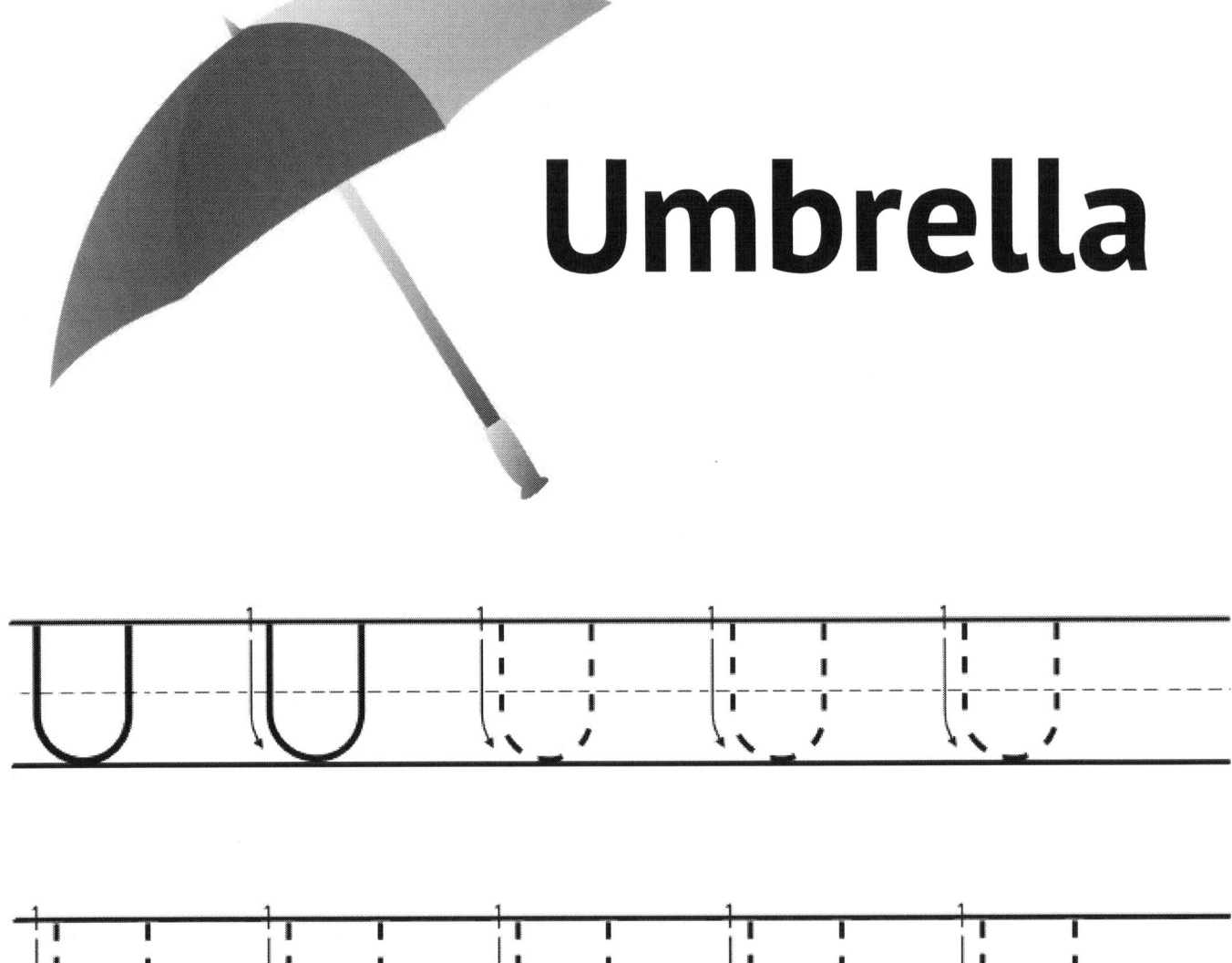

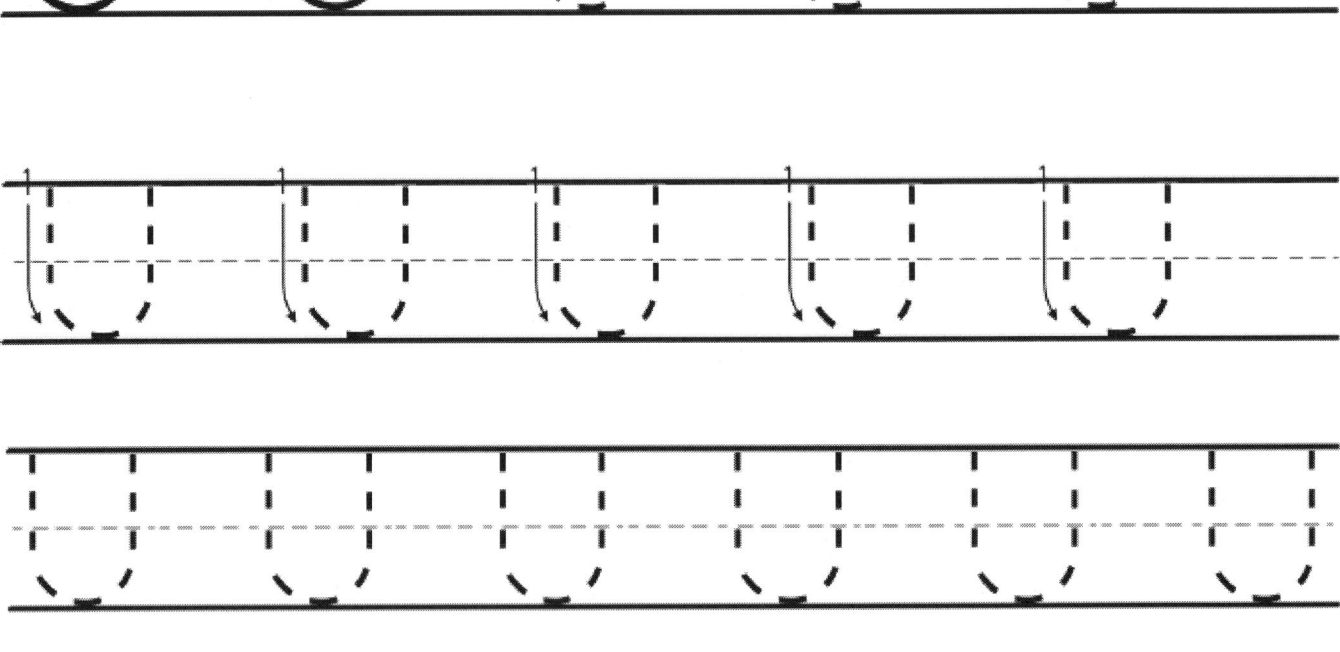

# UFO

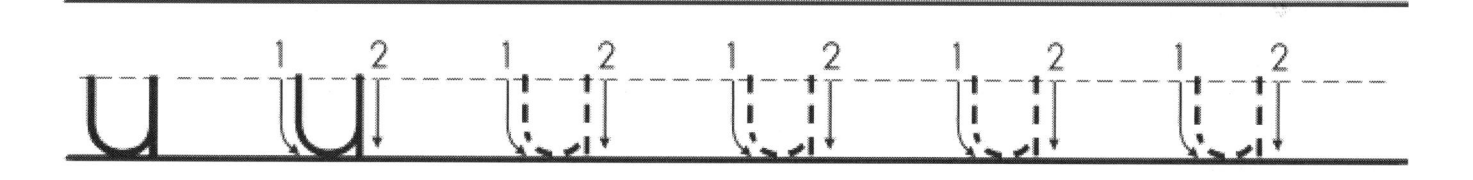

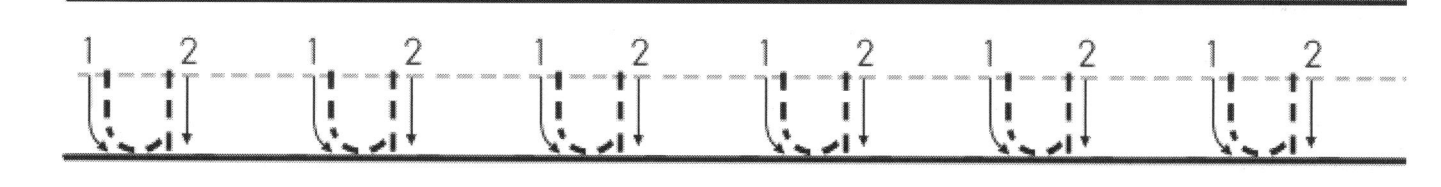

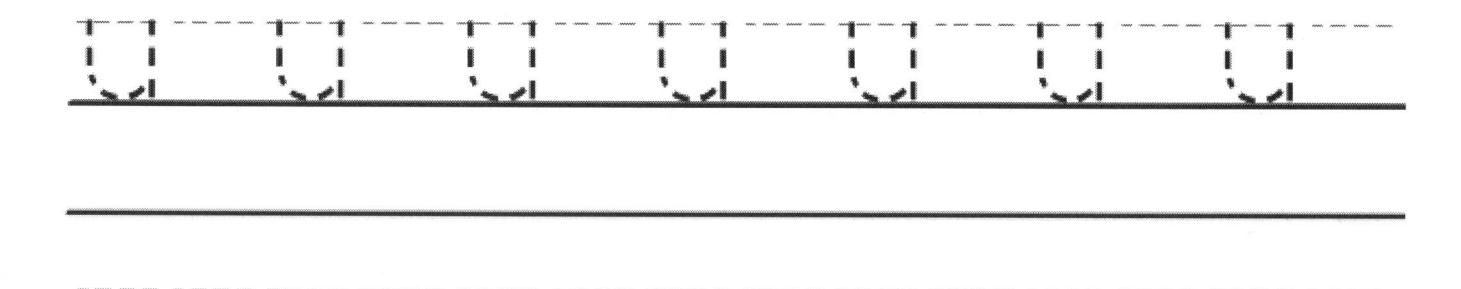

# Vulture

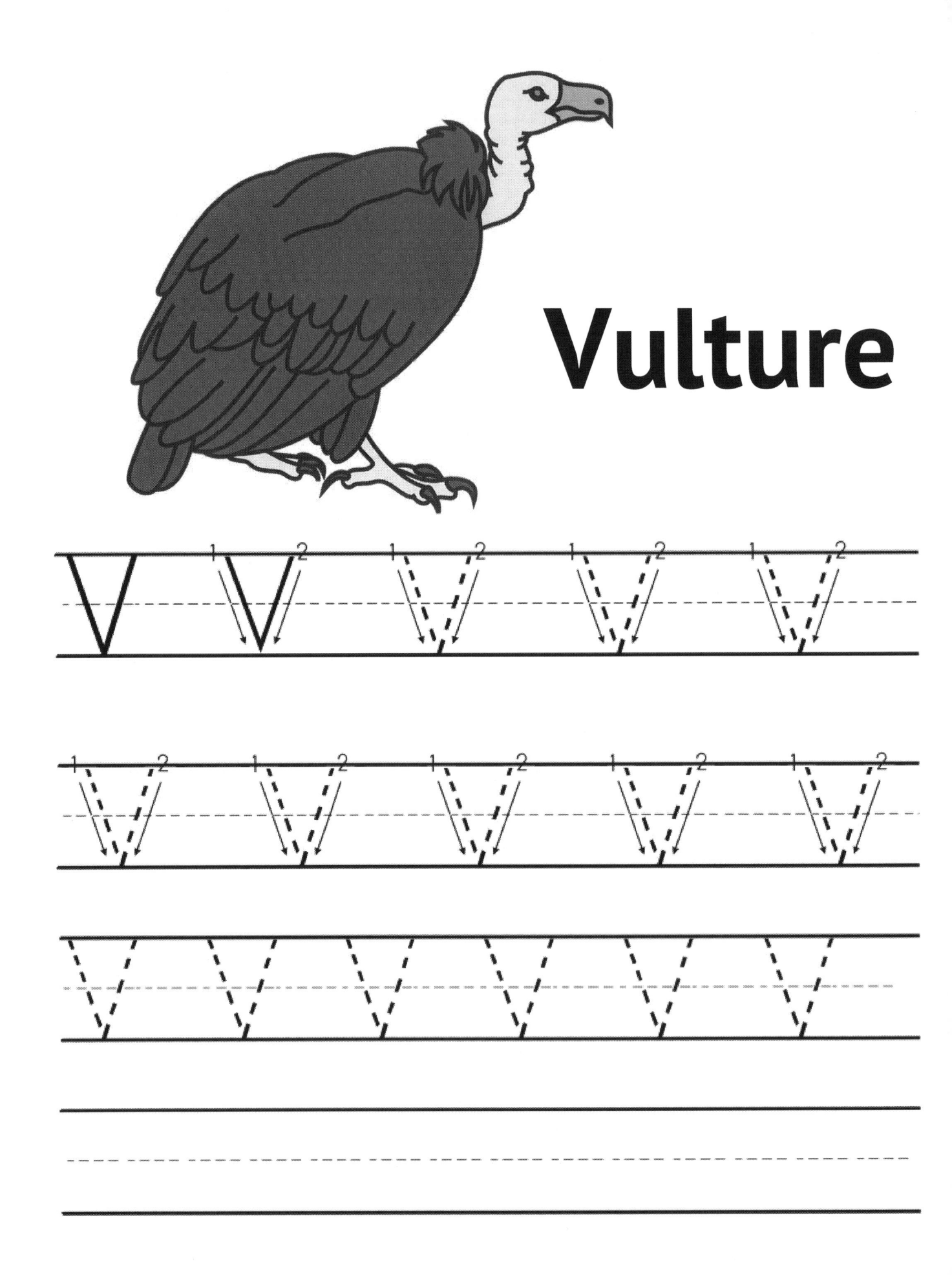

# Violin

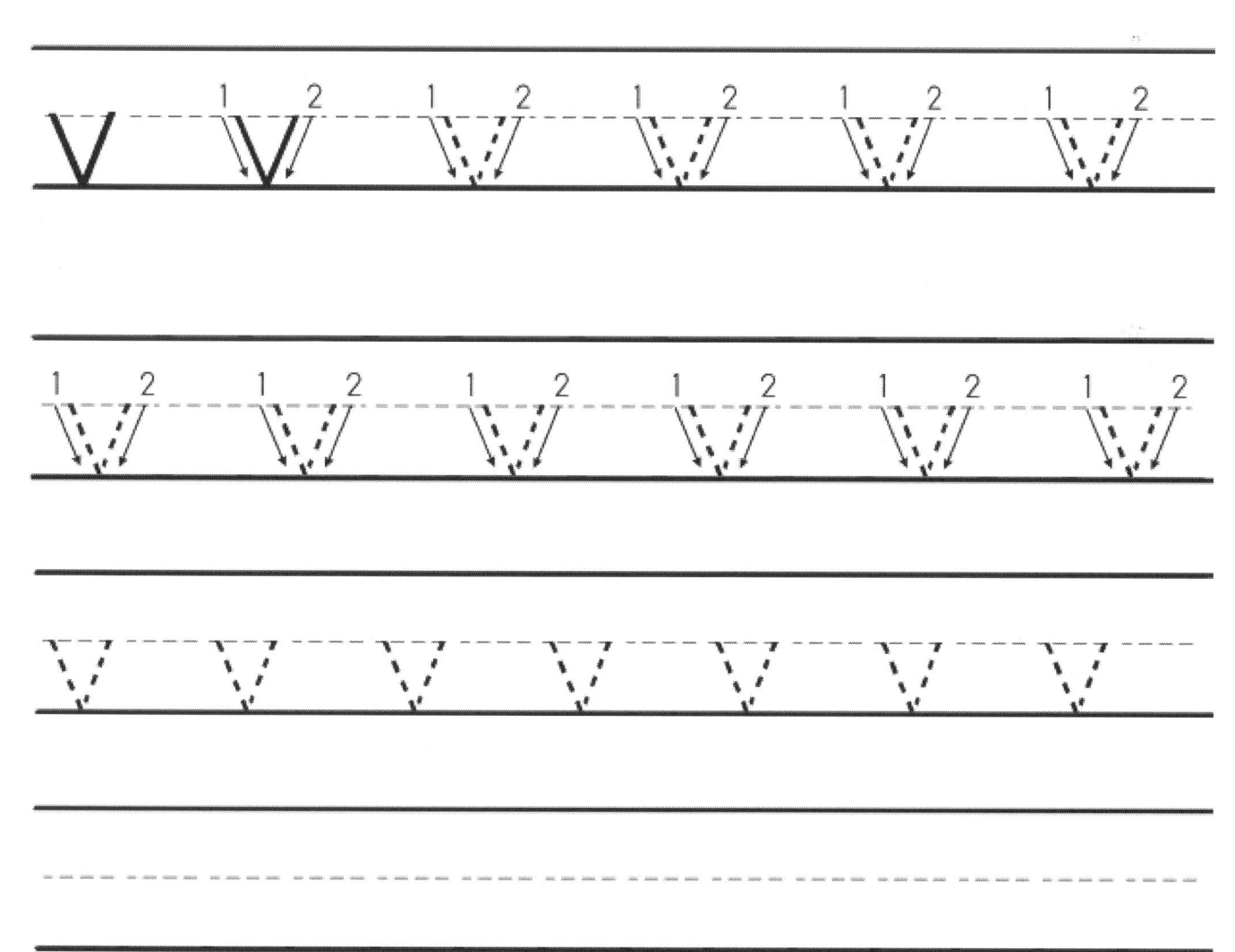

# Whale

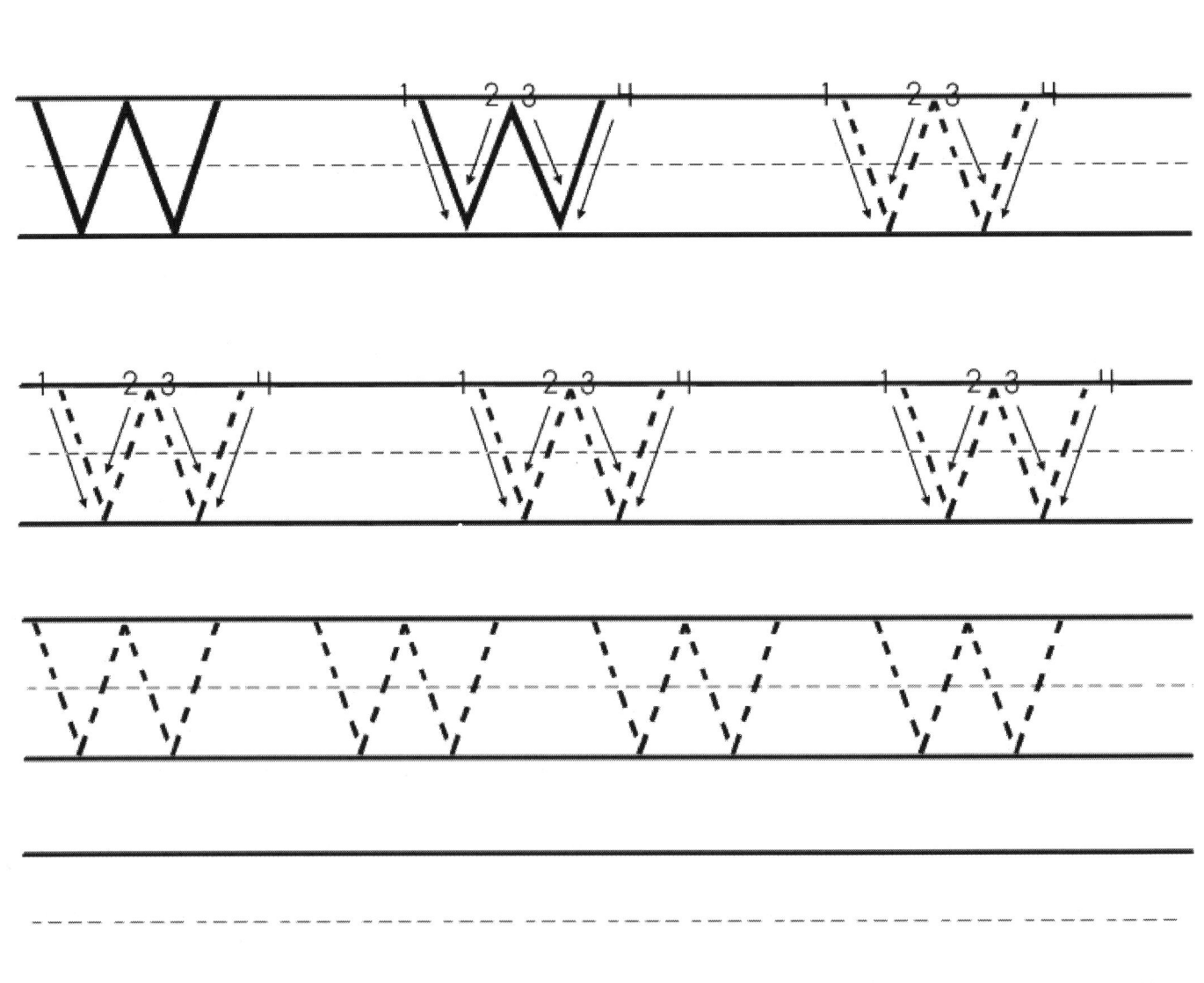

# Windows

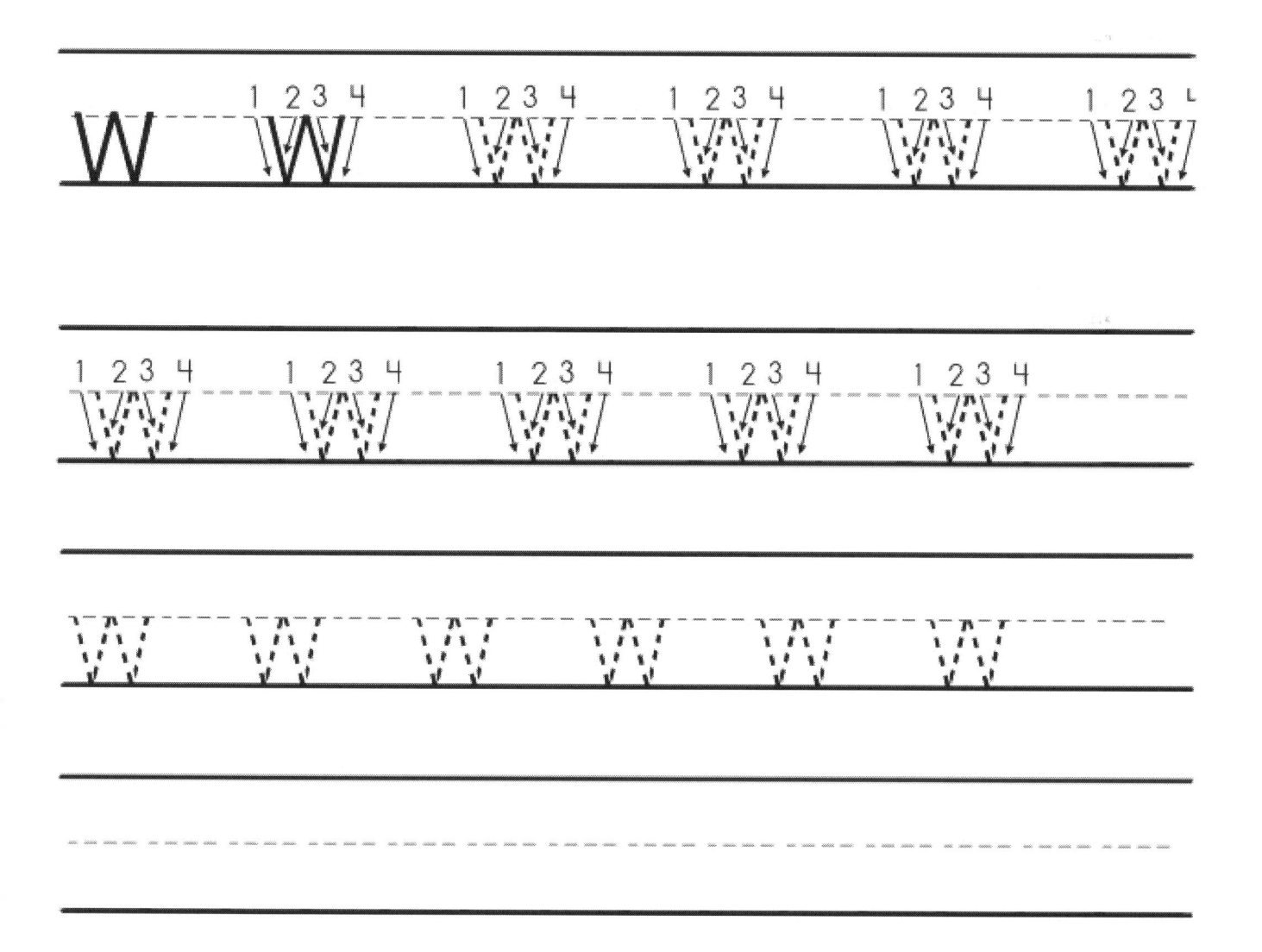

W  W  W  W  W  W

W  W  W  W  W

w  w  w  w  w  w

# Xmas

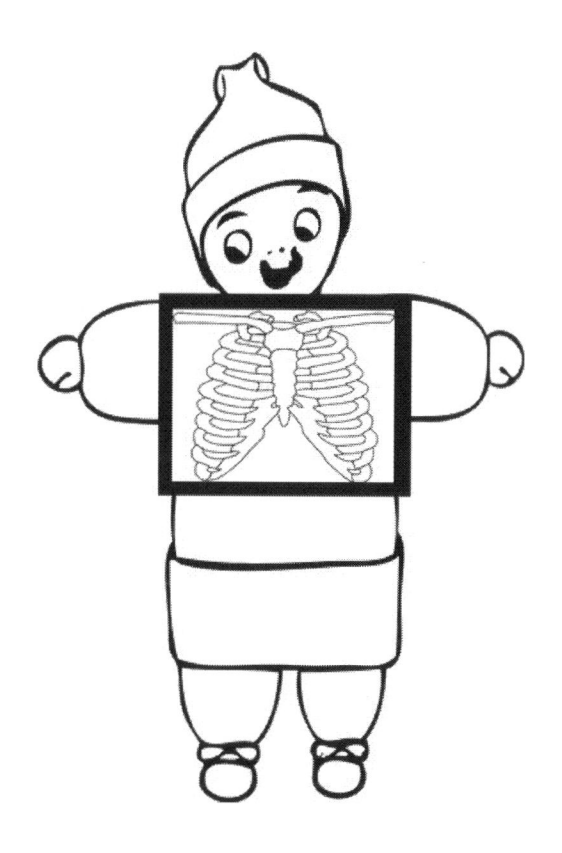

# X-ray

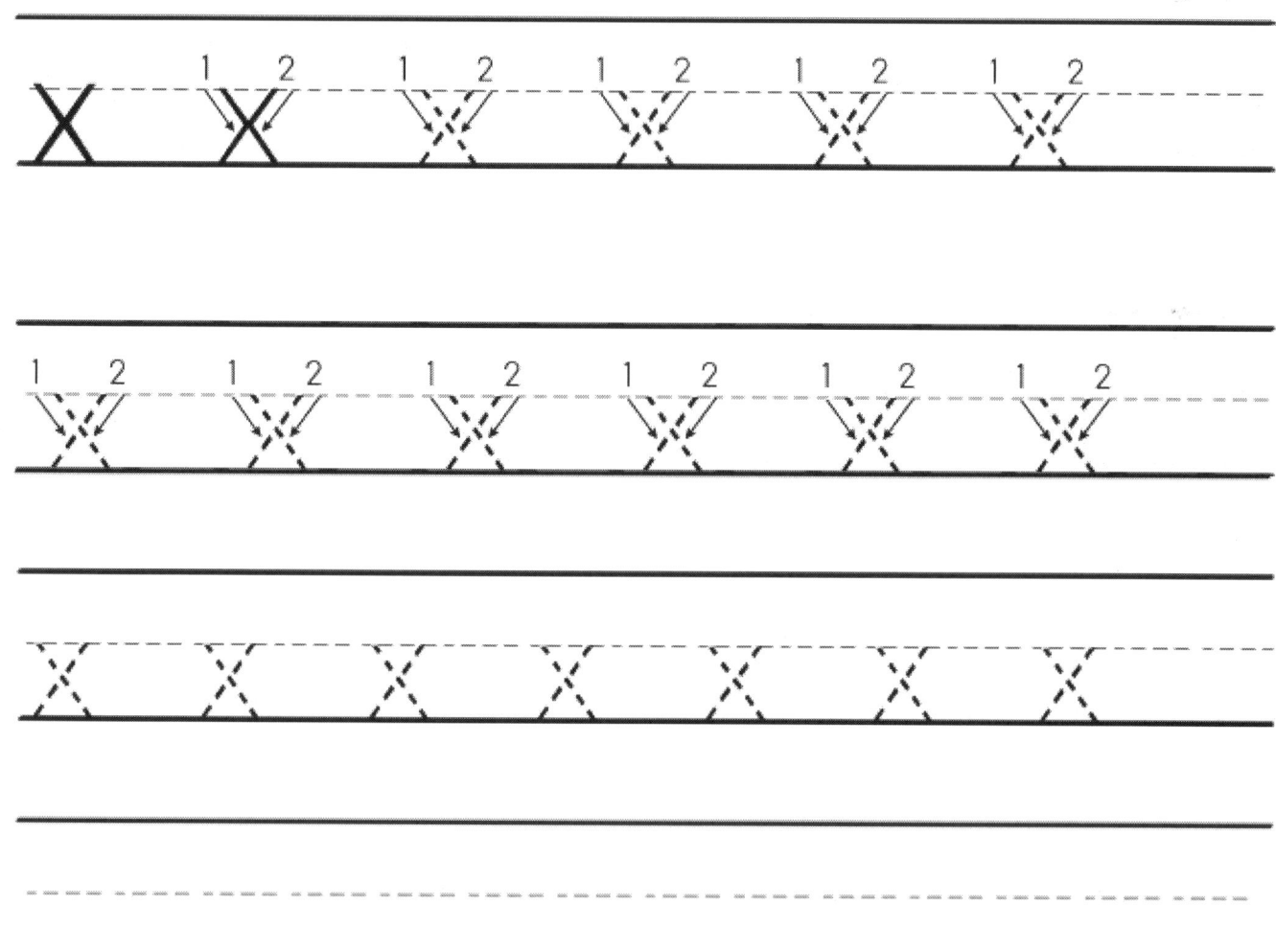

# Yacht

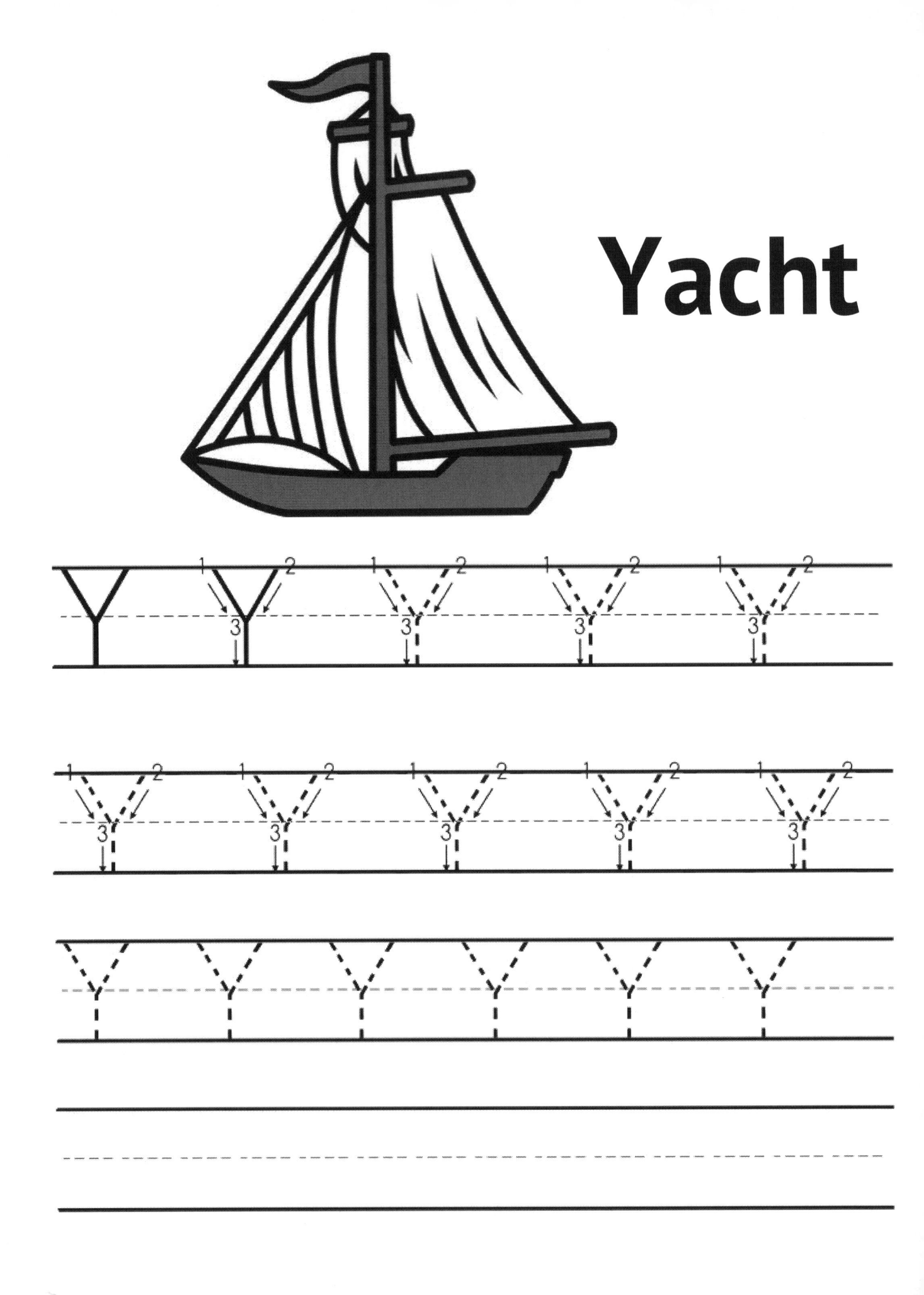

# Yarn

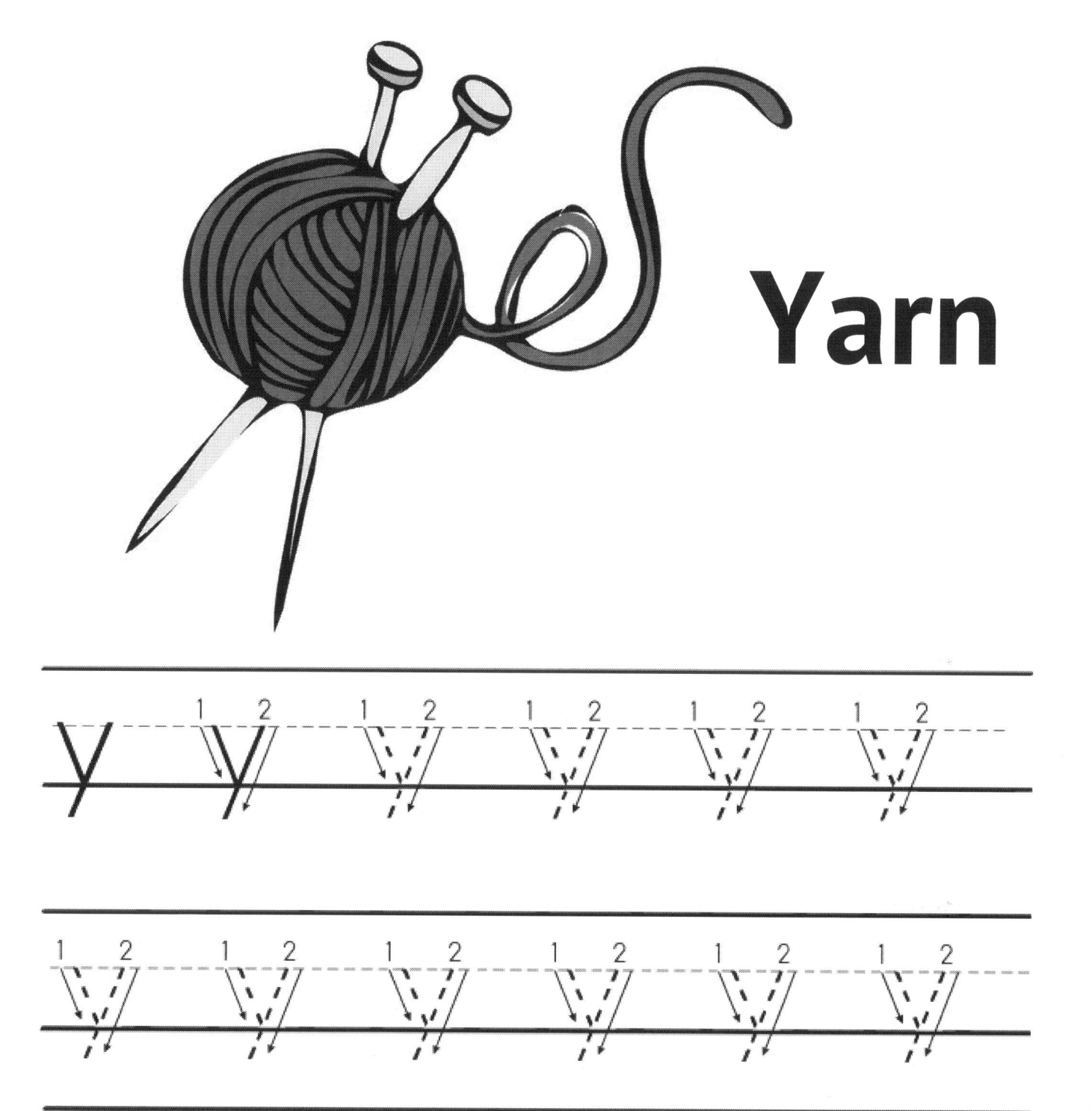

# Zebra

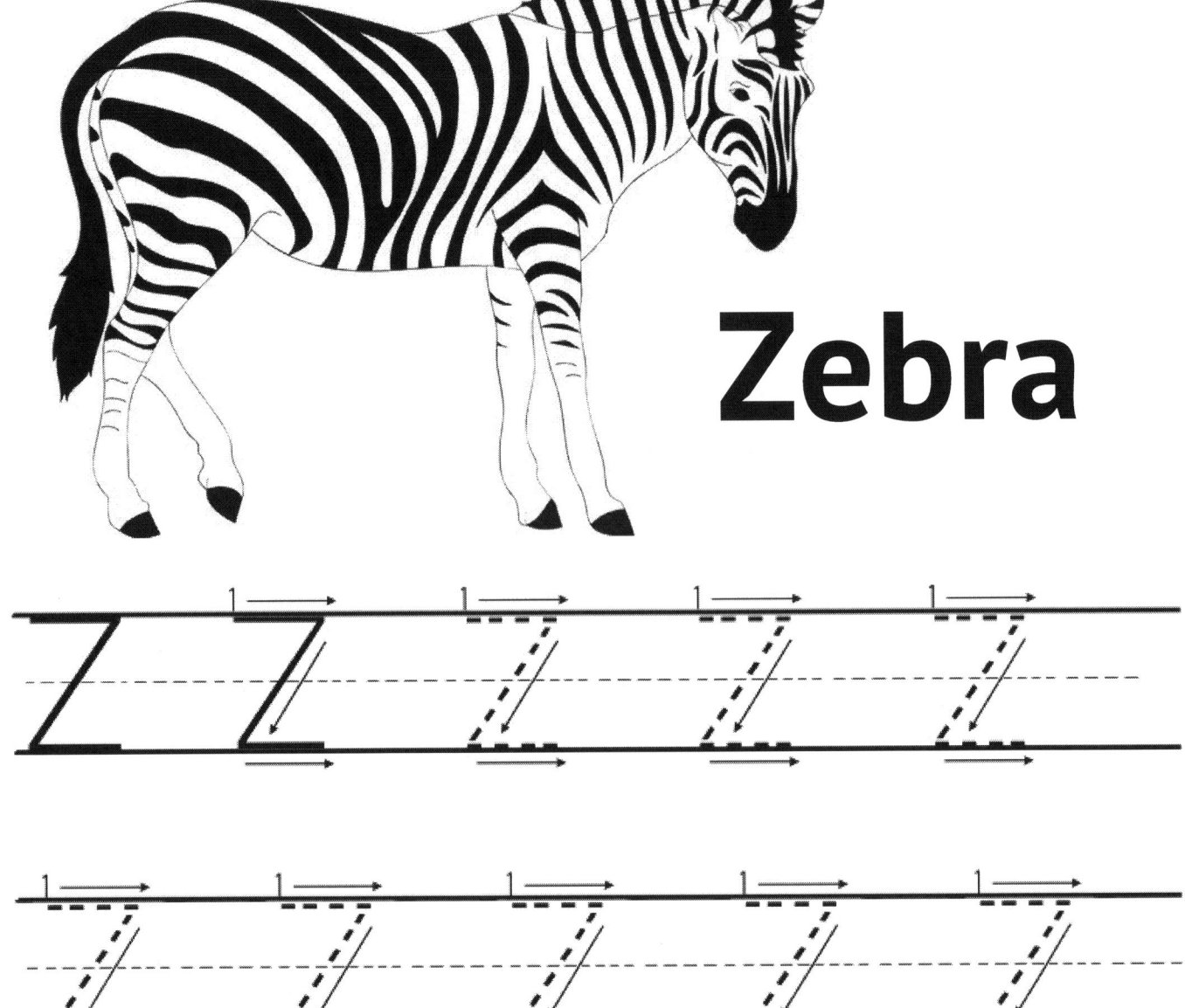

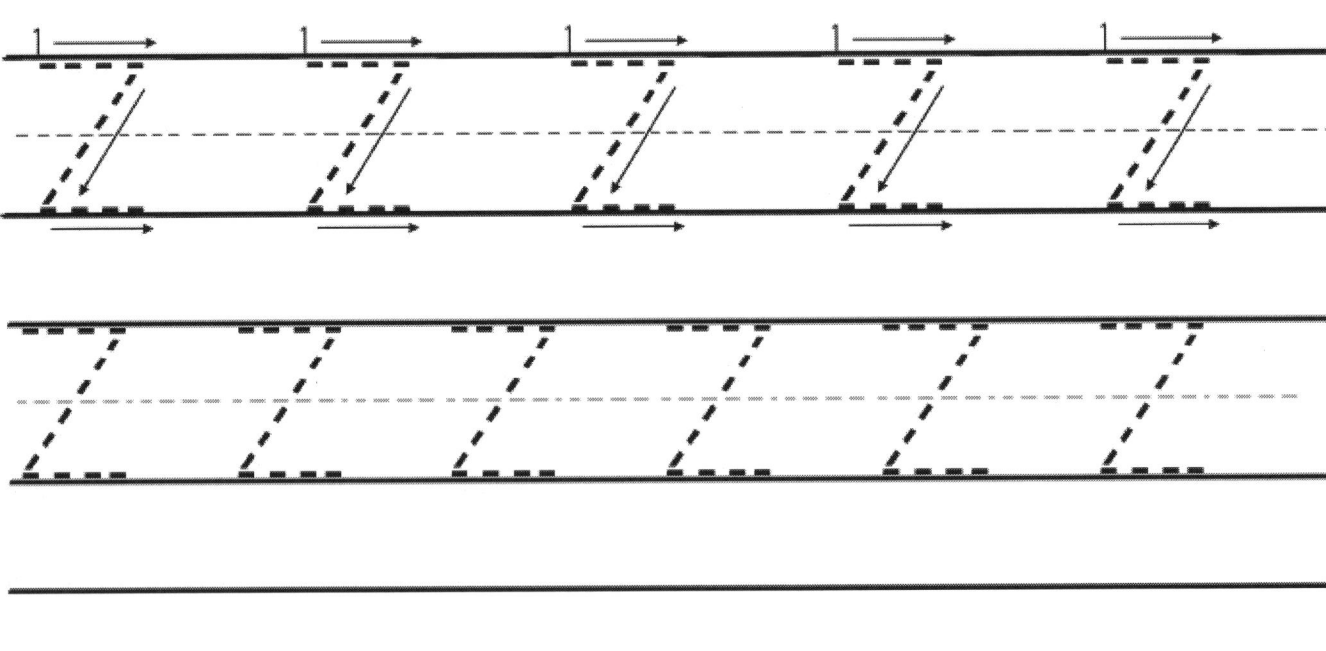

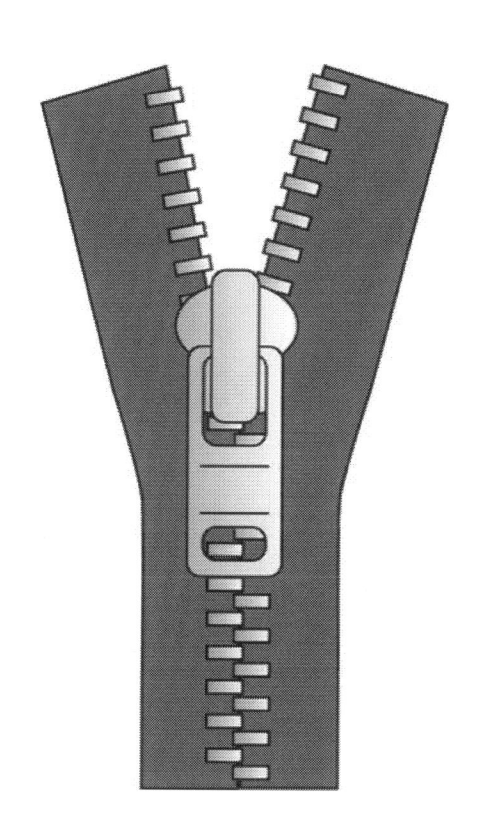

# Zip

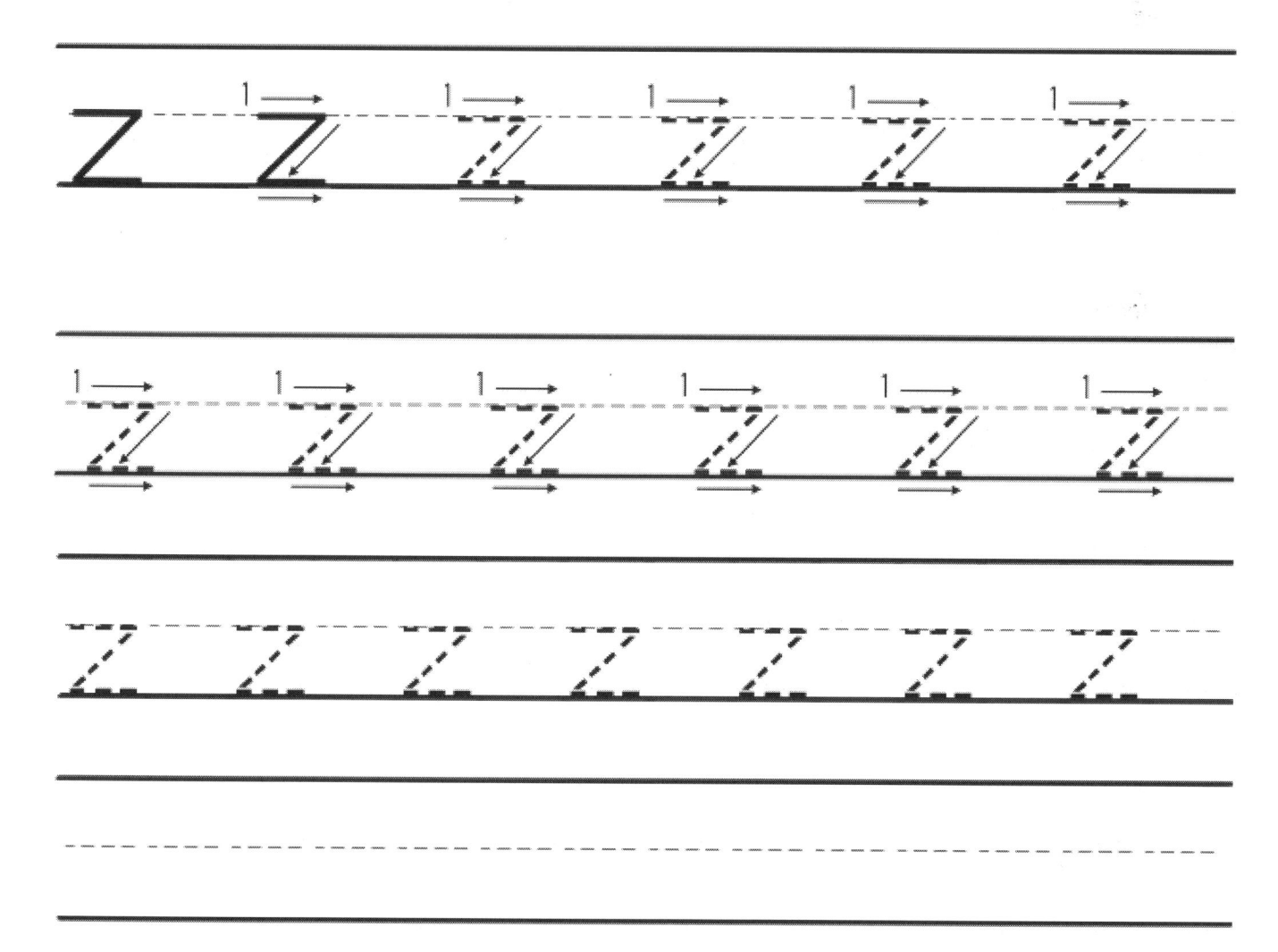

# Part2 : Easy Word Tracing

# Ant

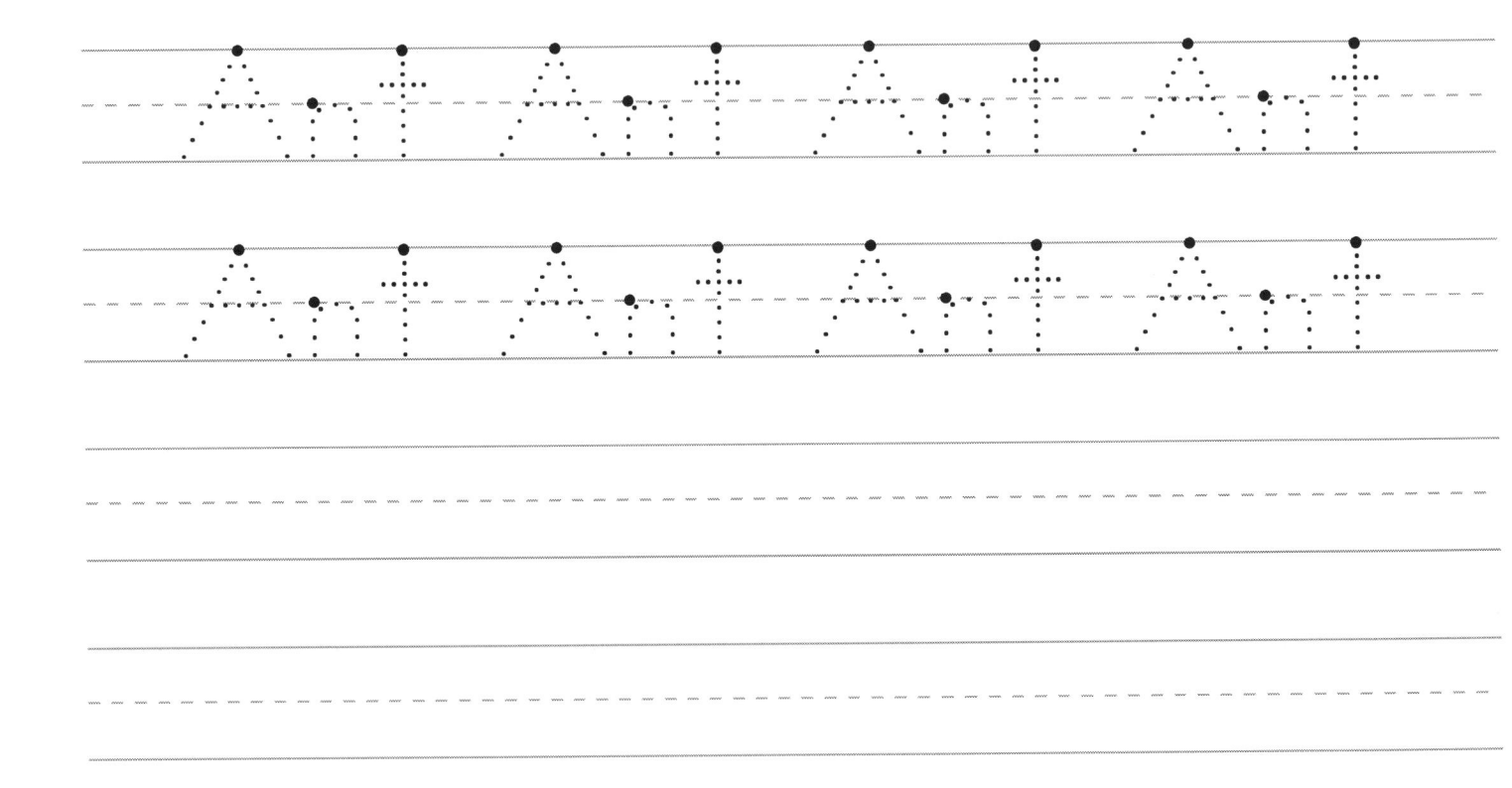

Ant Ant Ant Ant

Ant Ant Ant Ant

# Airplane

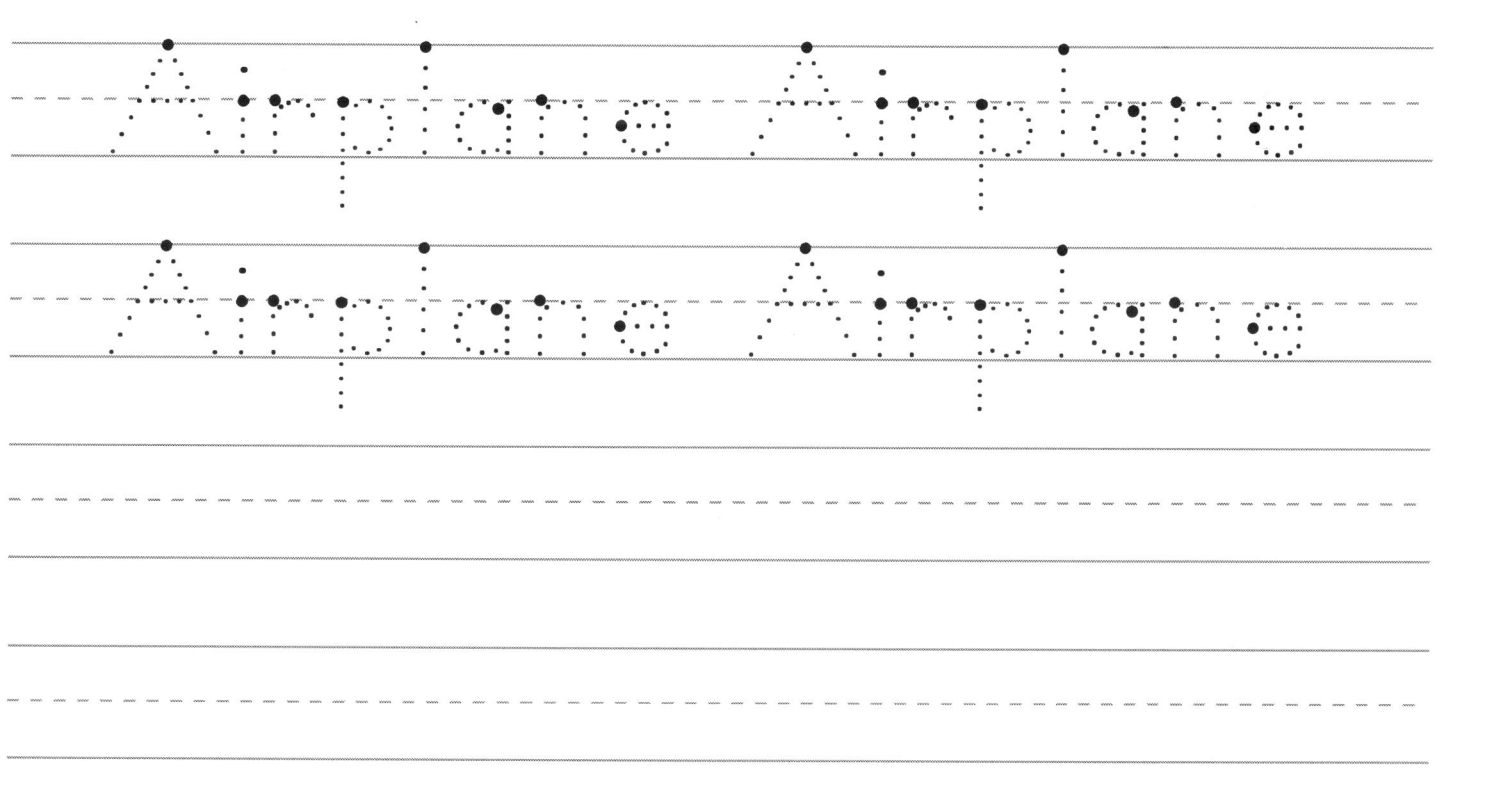

Airplane Airplane

Airplane Airplane

# Boat

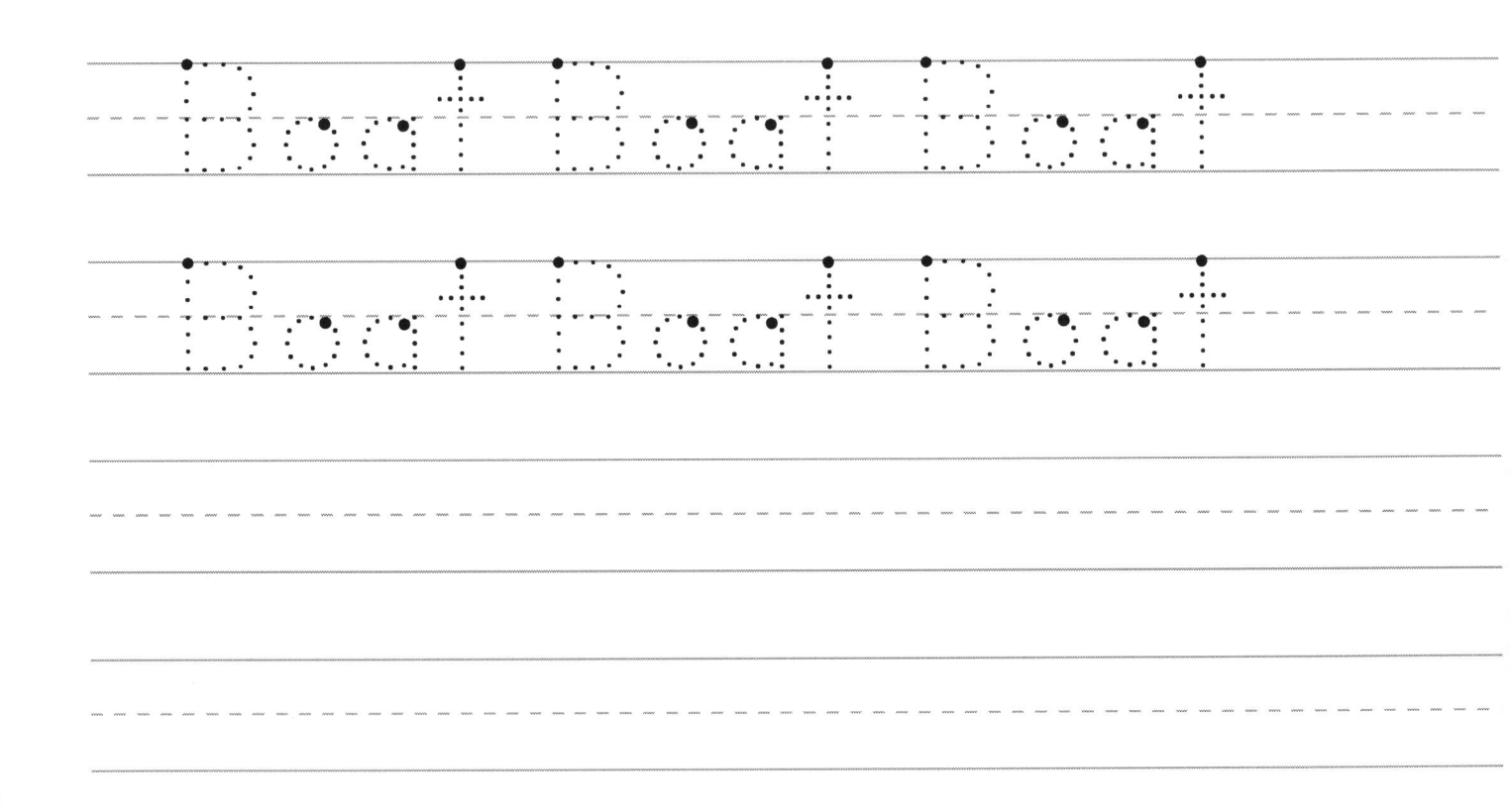

Boat Boat Boat

Boat Boat Boat

# Bicycle

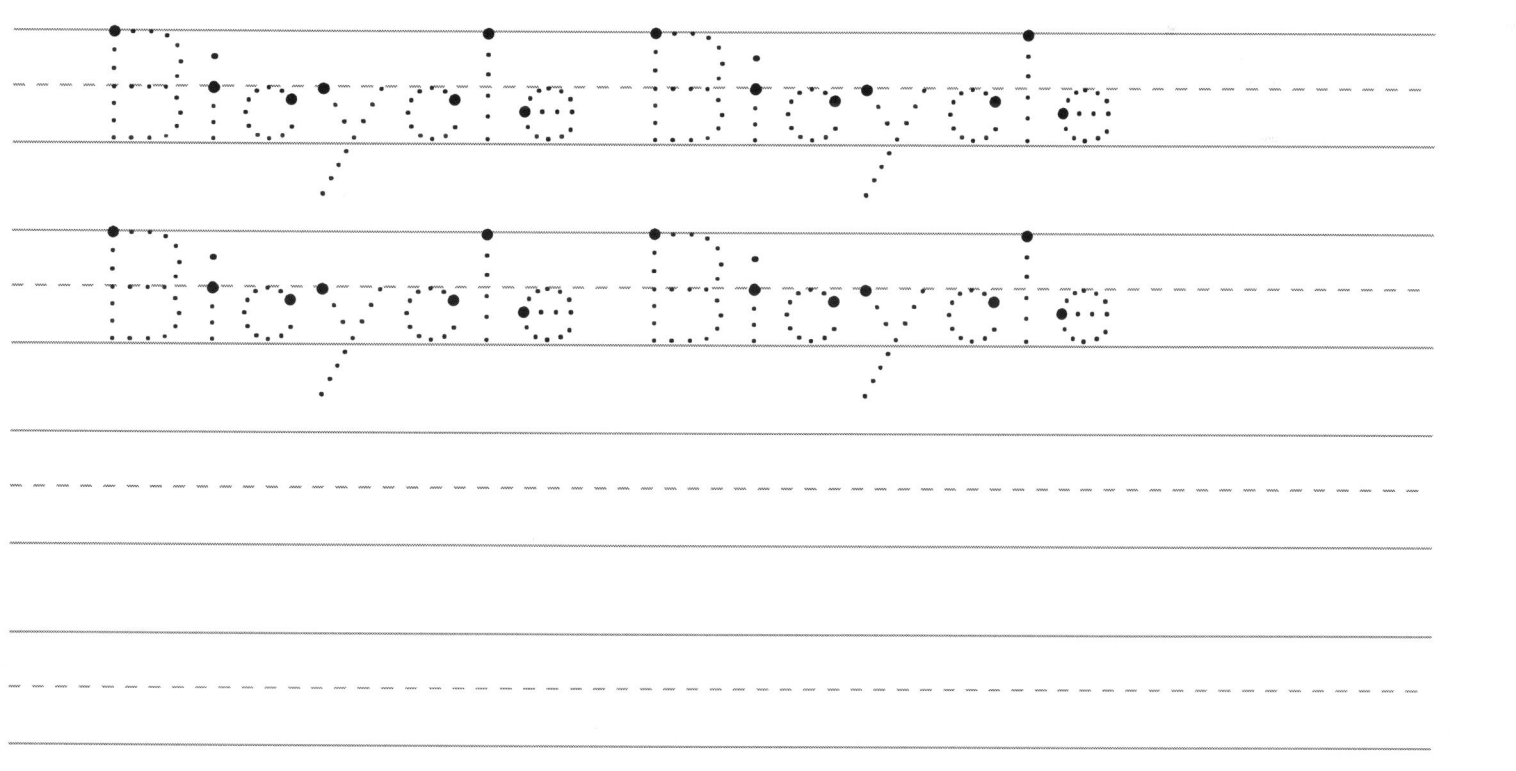

Bicycle Bicycle

Bicycle Bicycle

# Cow

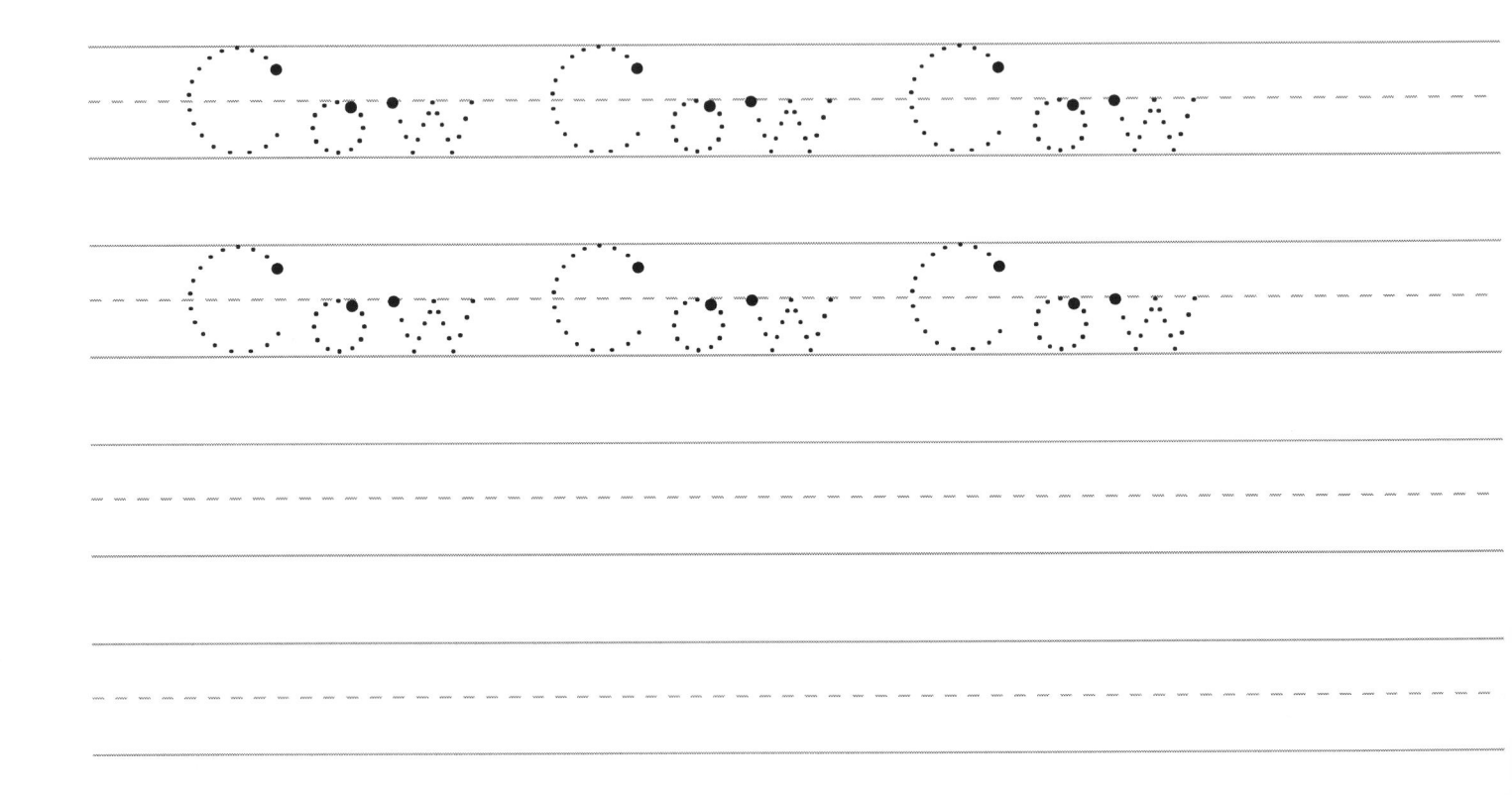

Cow Cow Cow

Cow Cow Cow

# Cat

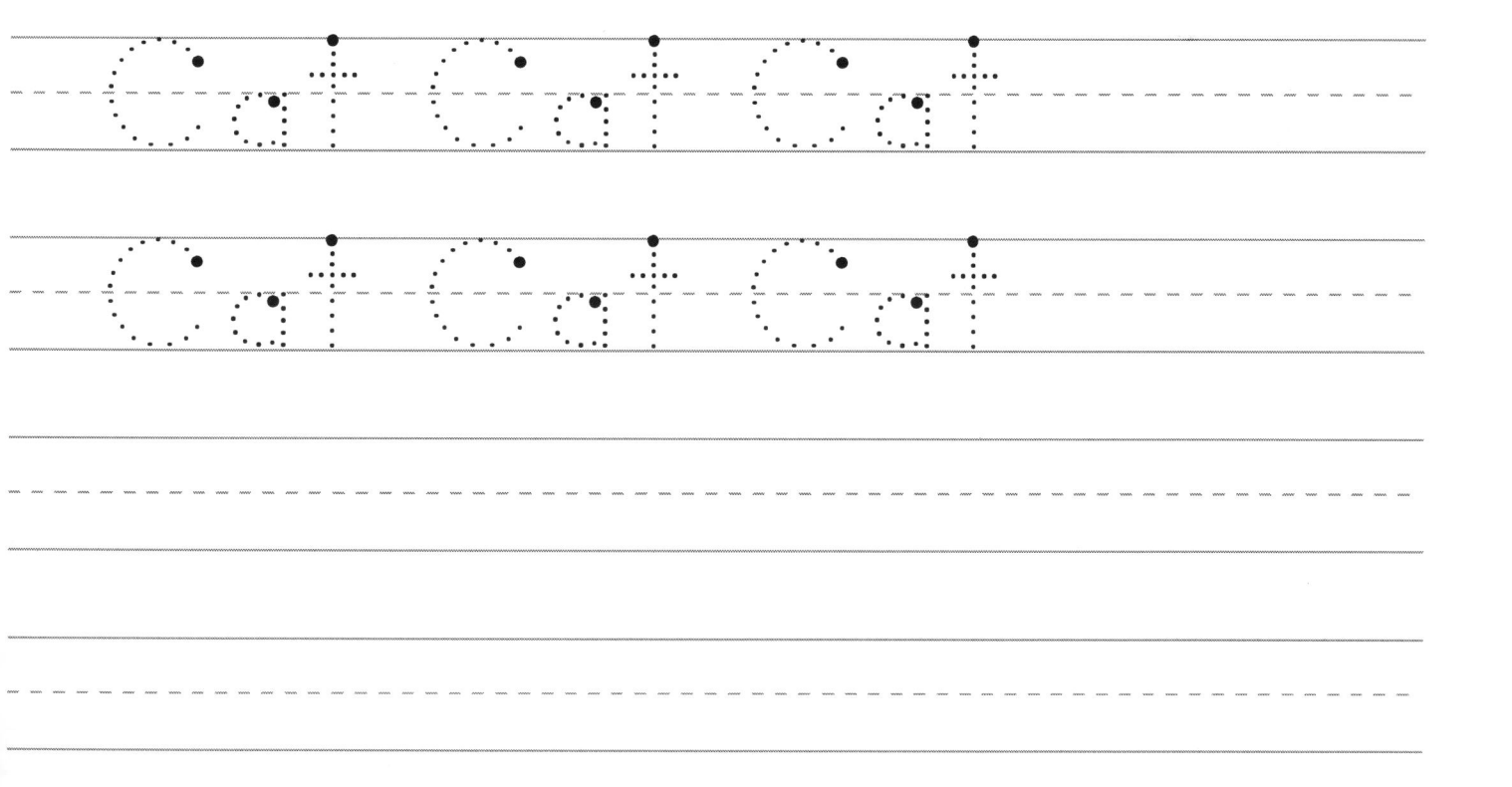

Cat Cat Cat

Cat Cat Cat

# Dinosaur

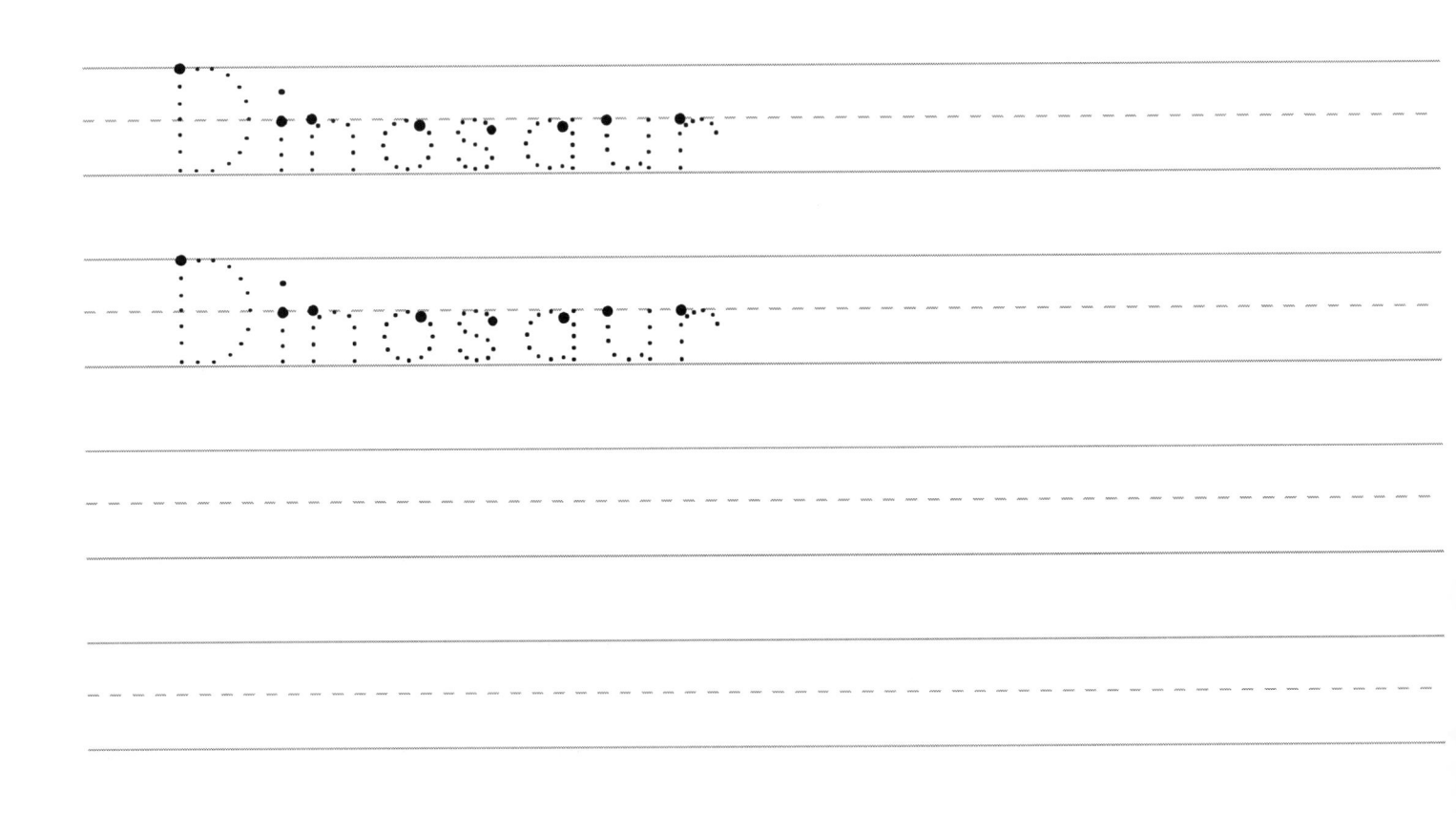

Dinosaur

Dinosaur

# Dog

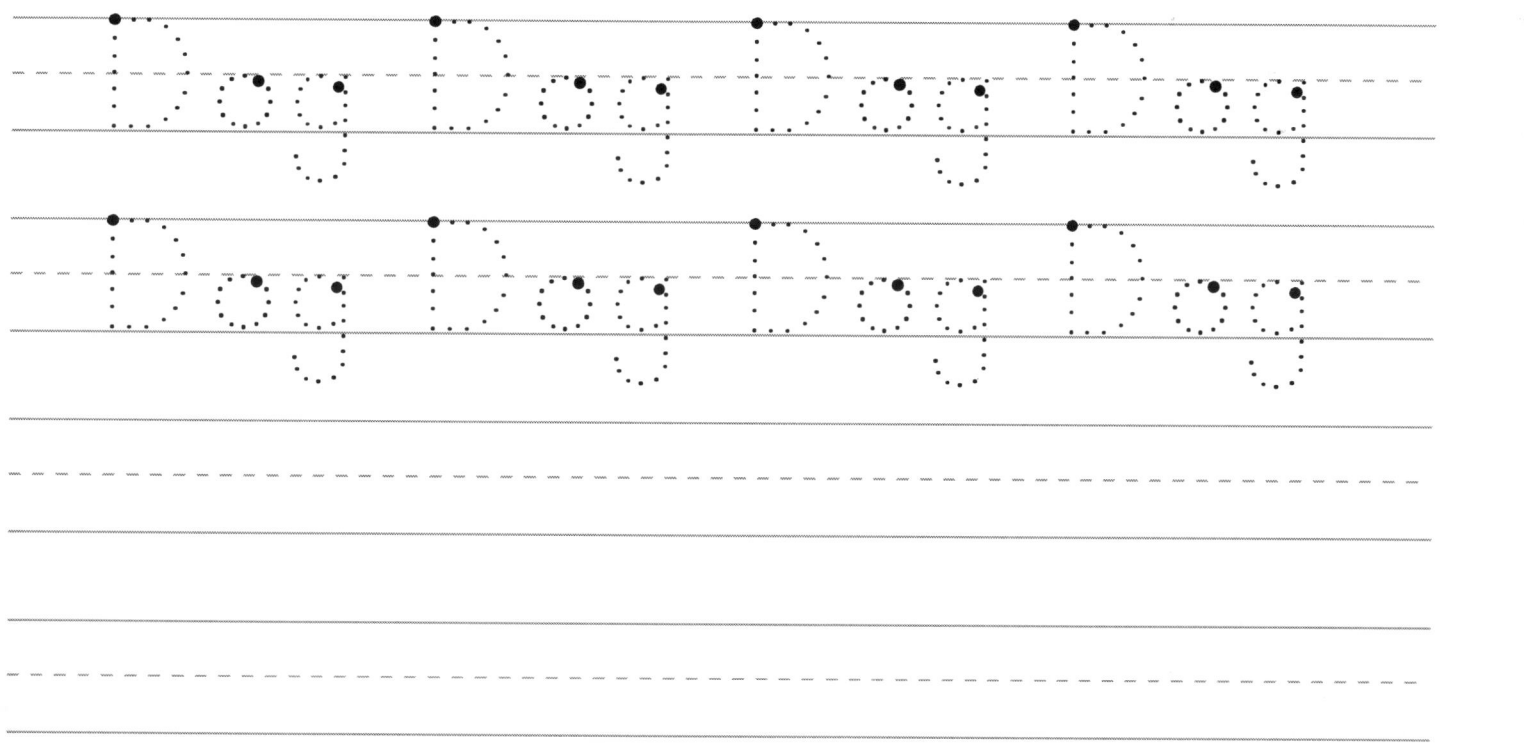

Dog Dog Dog Dog
Dog Dog Dog Dog

# Elephant

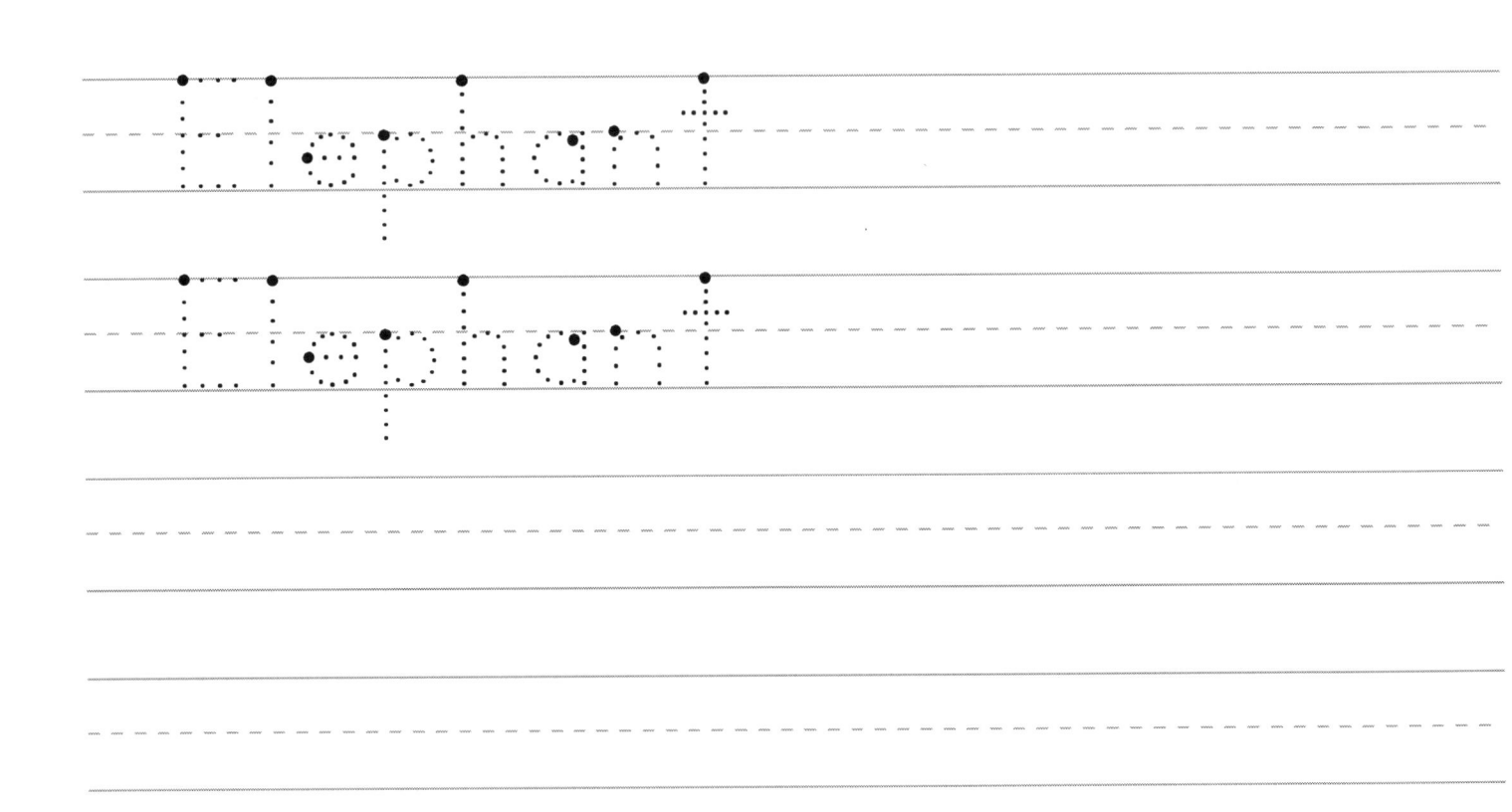

Elephant

Elephant

# Eagle

Eagle Eagle Eagle

Eagle Eagle Eagle

# Fox

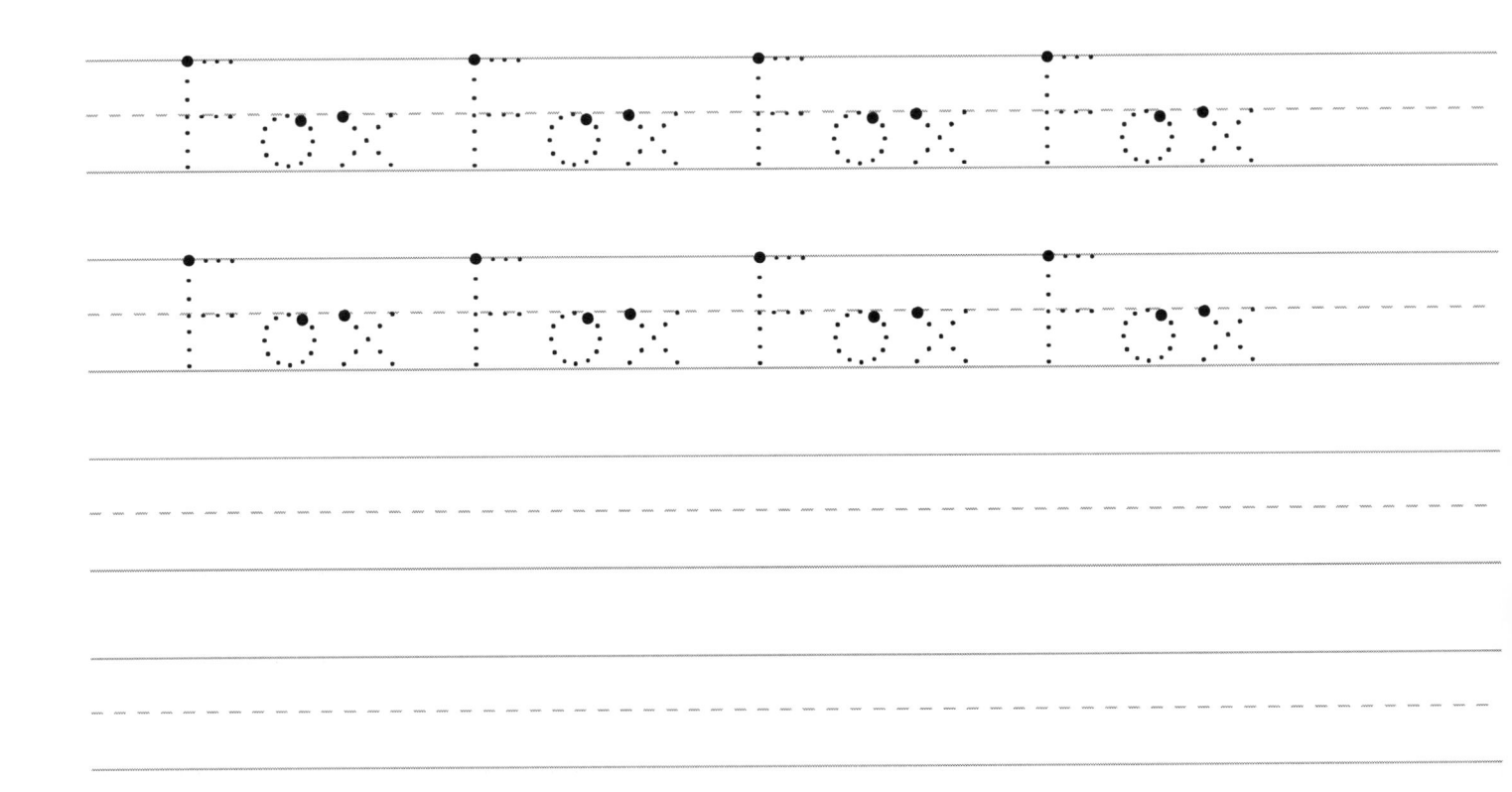

Fox Fox Fox Fox

Fox Fox Fox Fox

# Flower

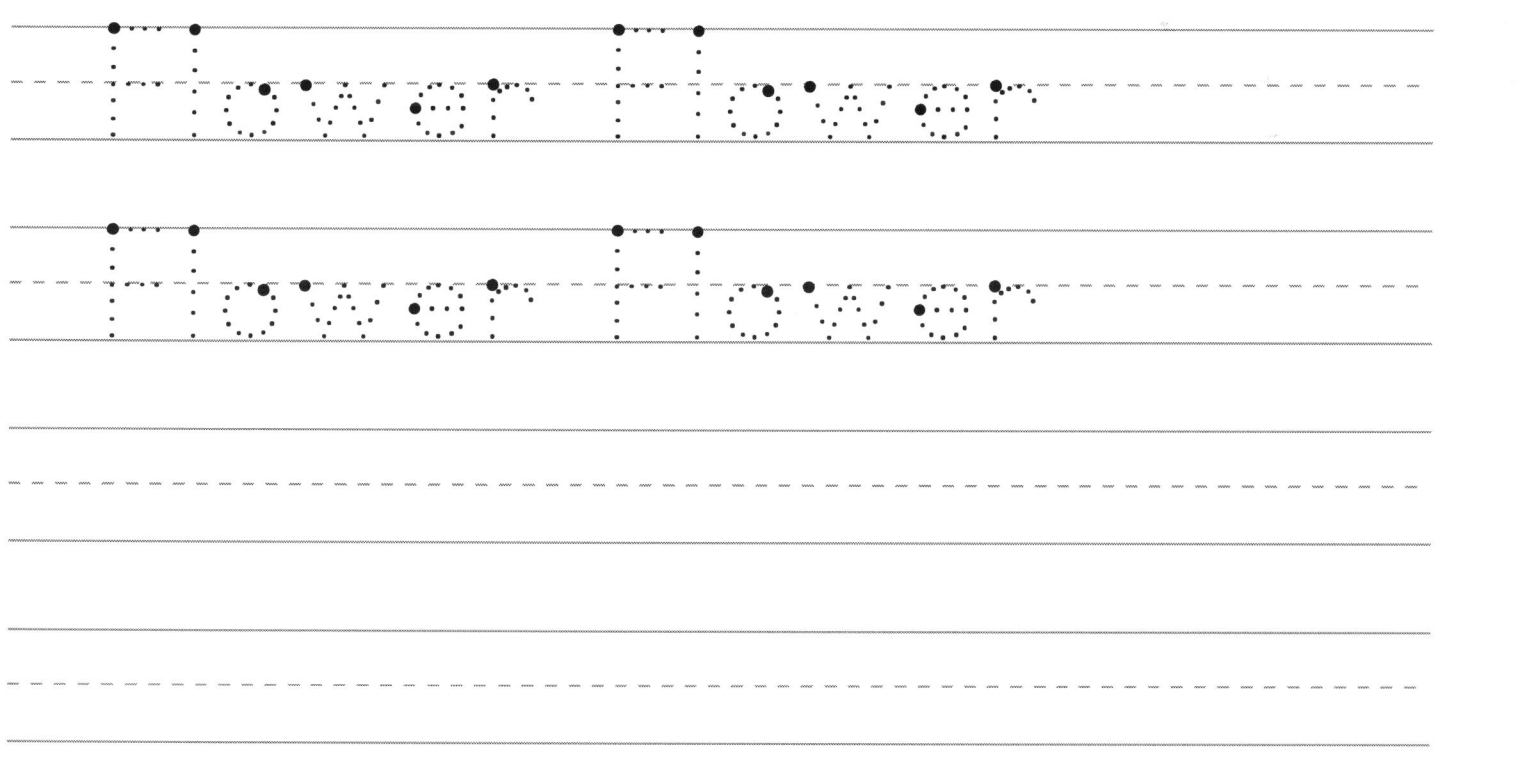

Flower Flower

Flower Flower

# Giraffe

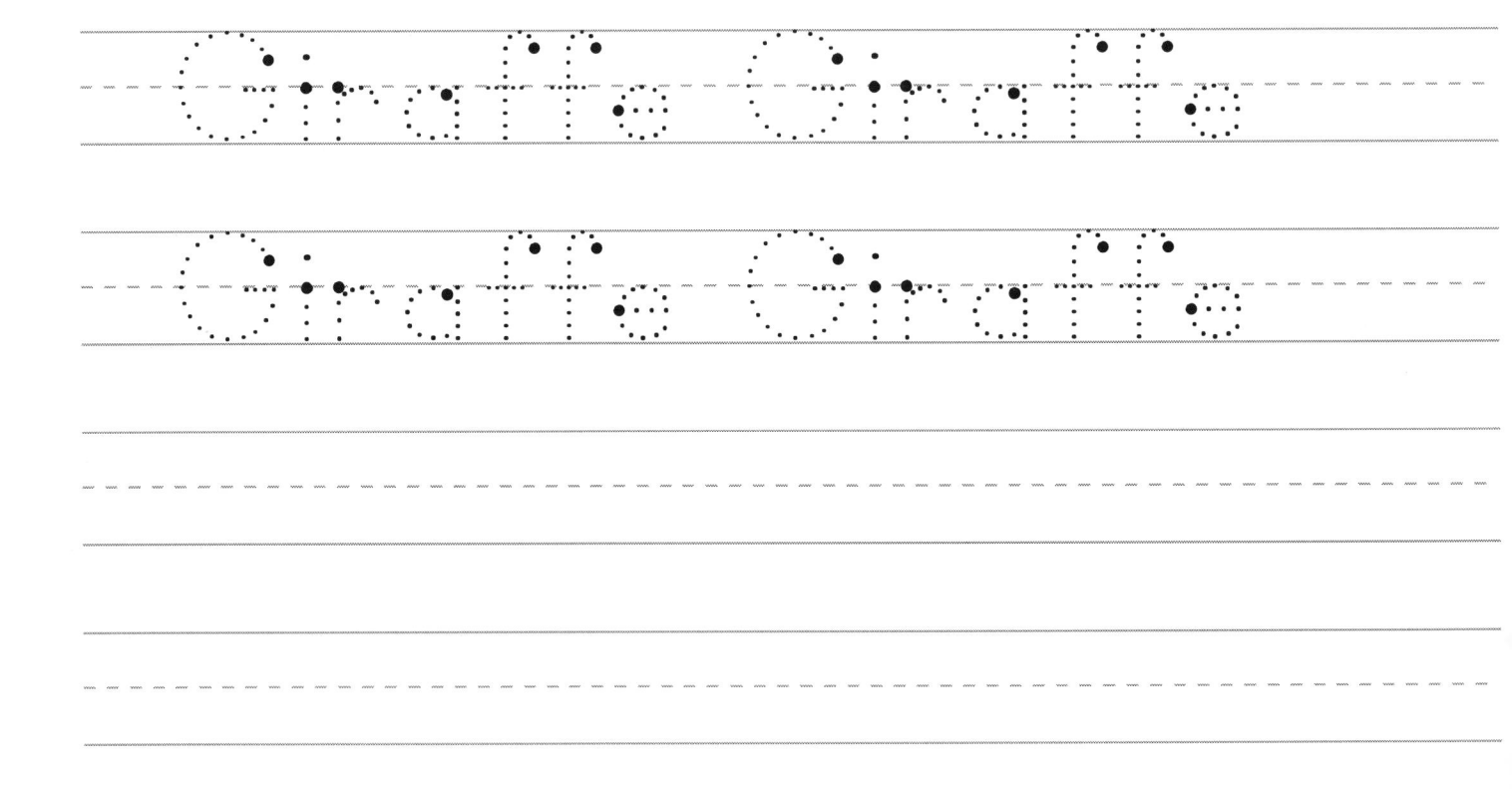

Giraffe Giraffe

Giraffe Giraffe

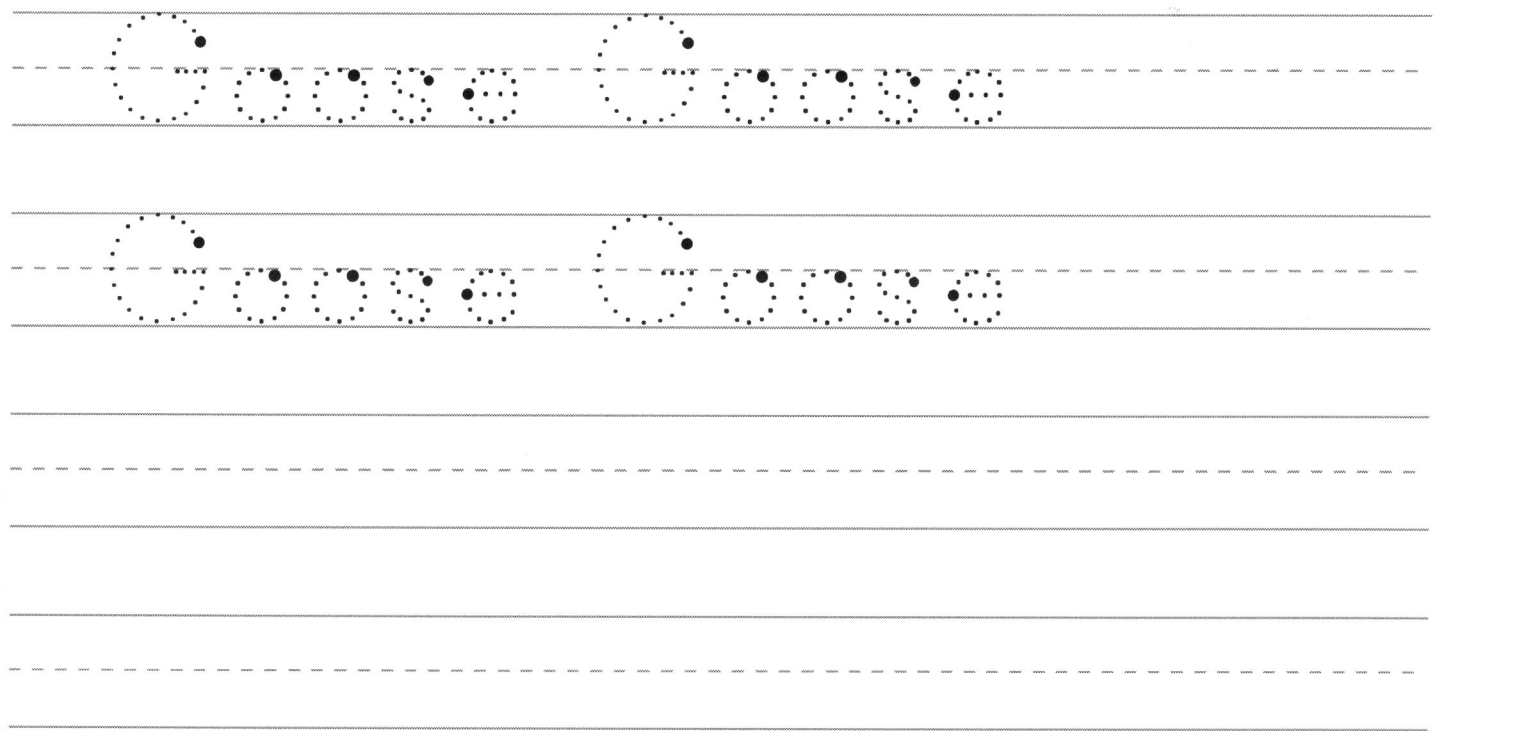

# Goose

Goose Goose

Goose Goose

# Hippopotamus

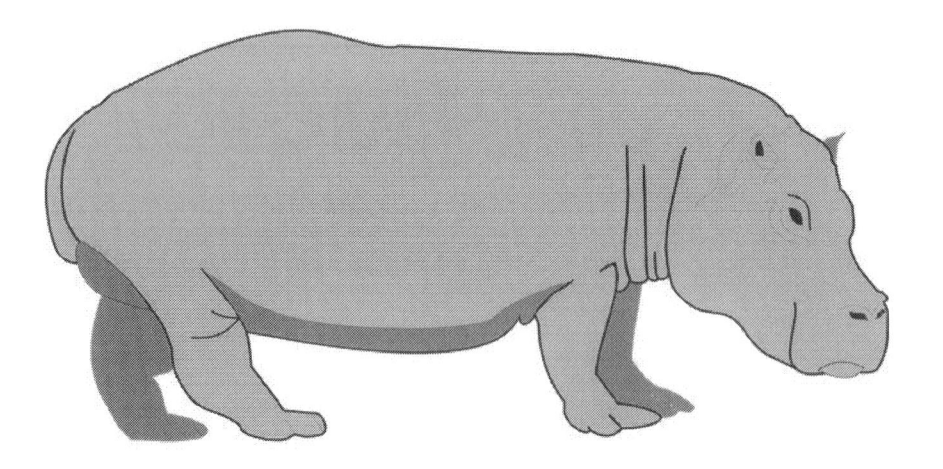

Hippopotamus

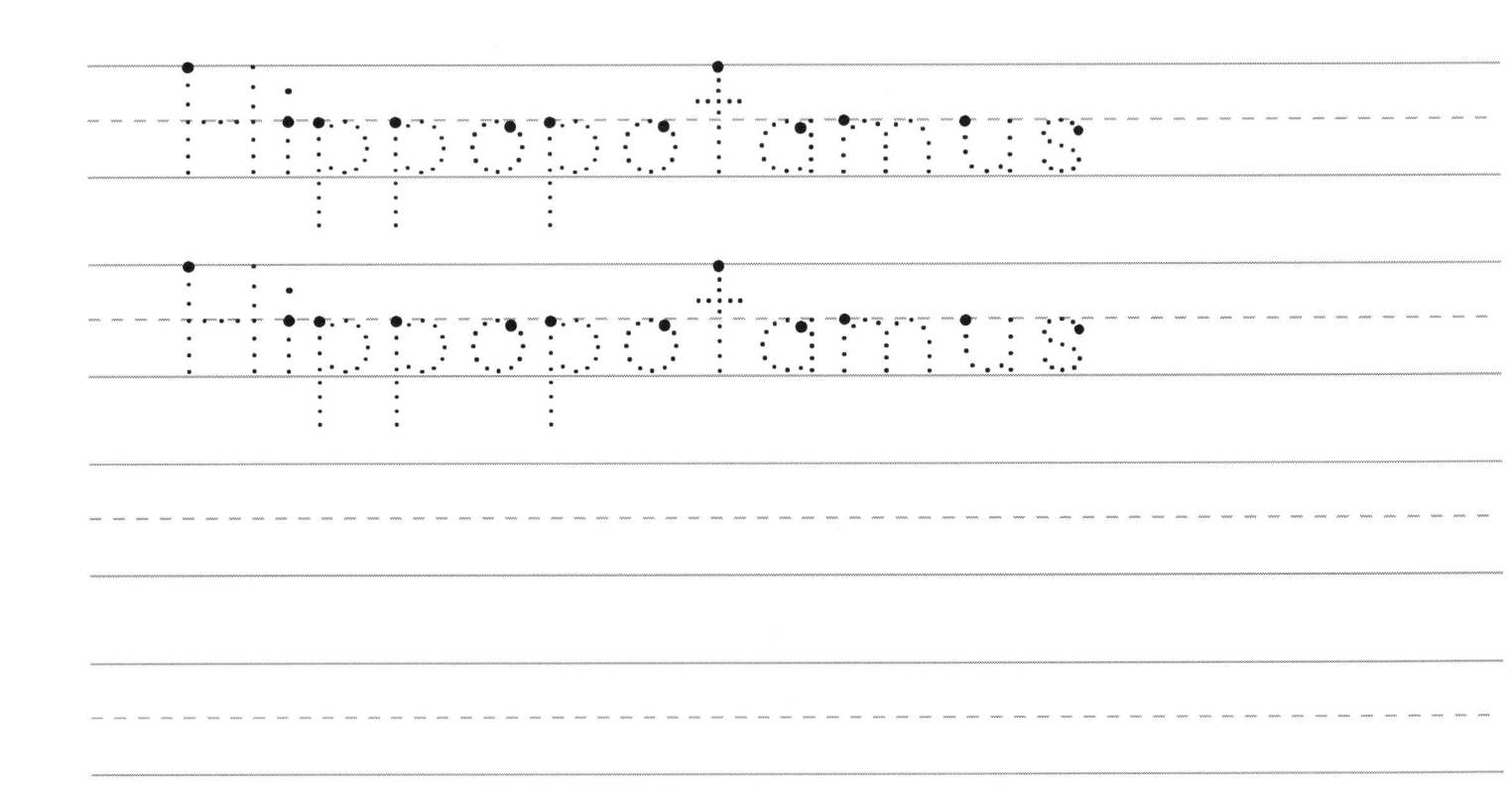

Hippopotamus

# Horse

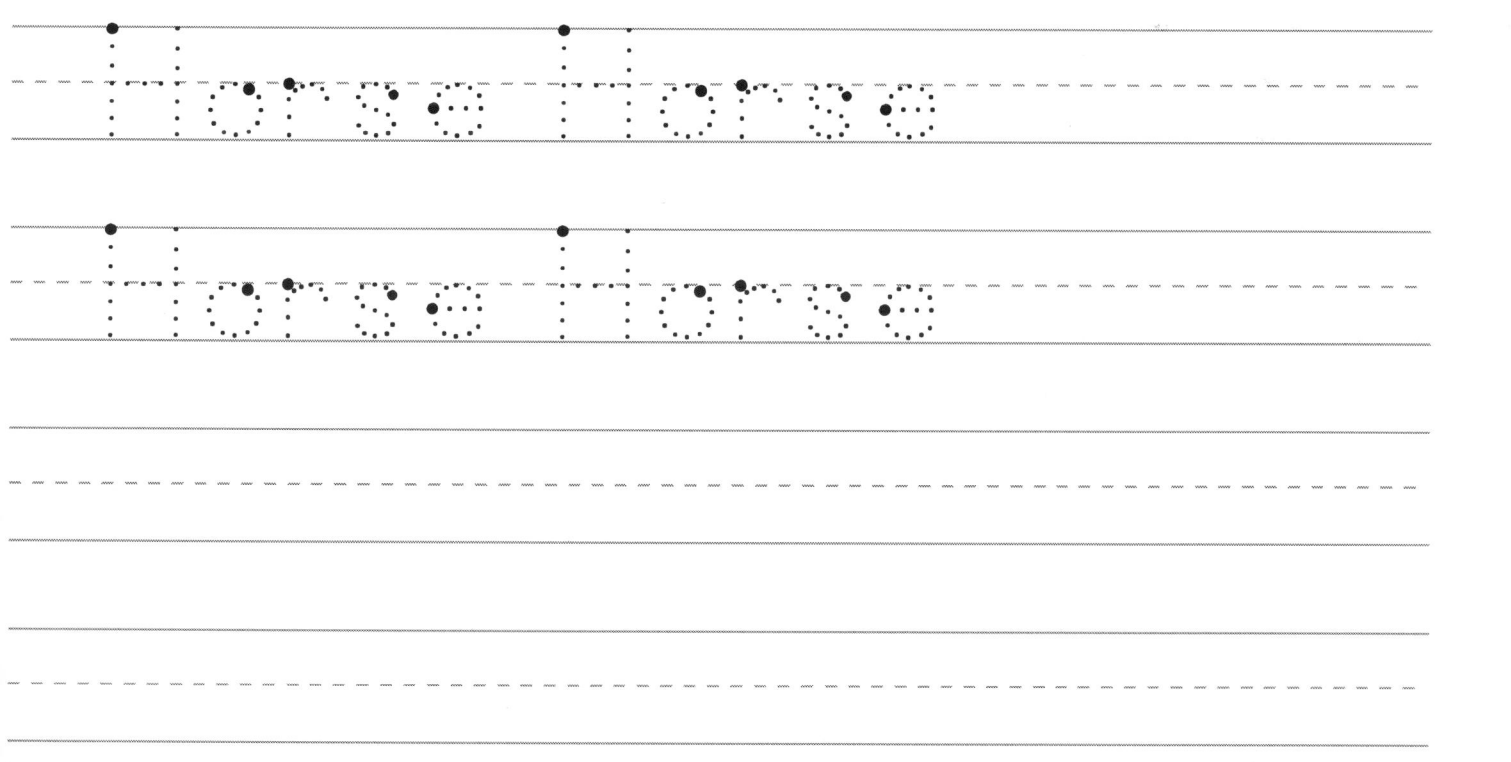

Horse Horse

Horse Horse

# I'm

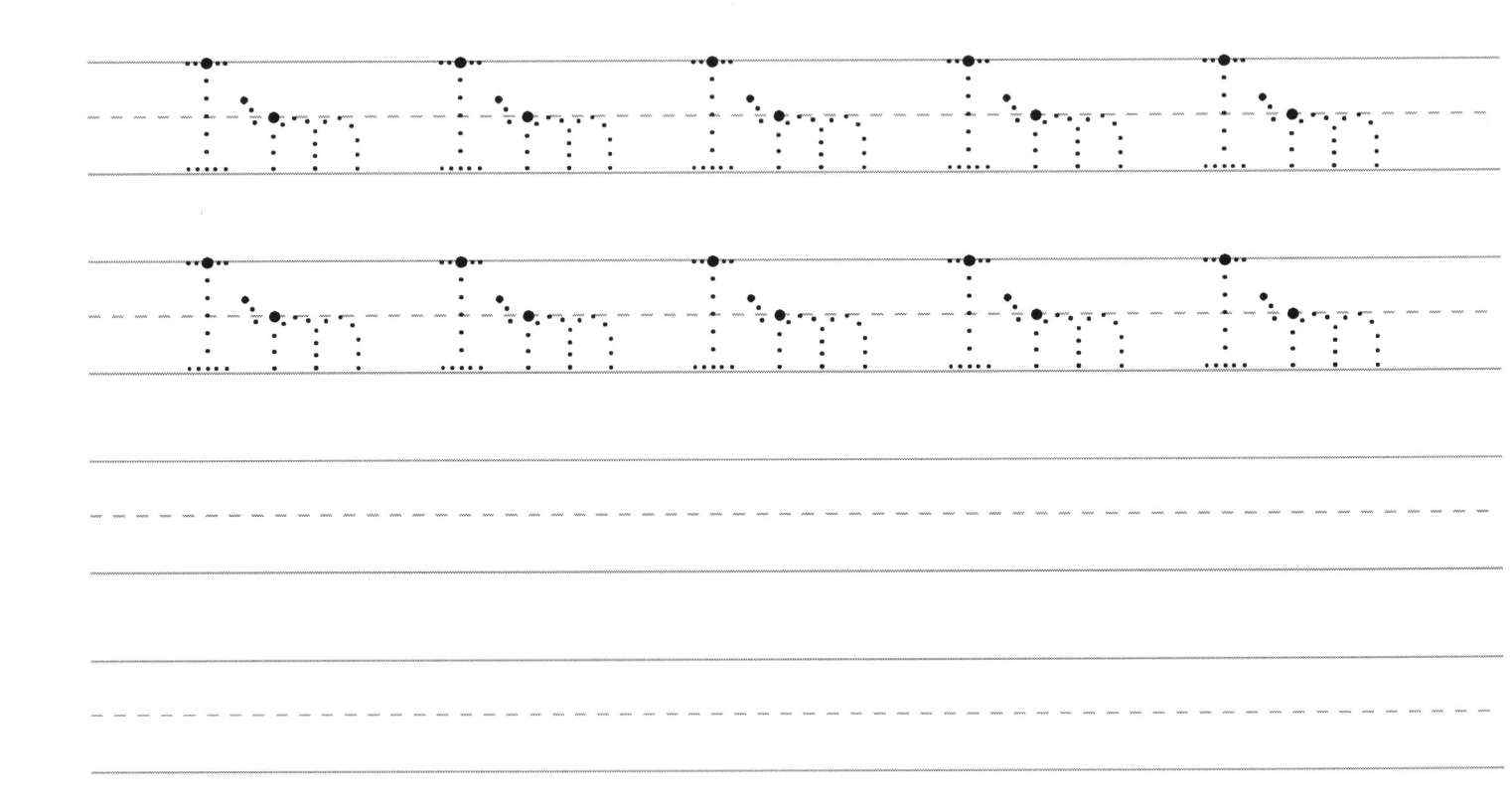

I'm I'm I'm I'm I'm

I'm I'm I'm I'm I'm

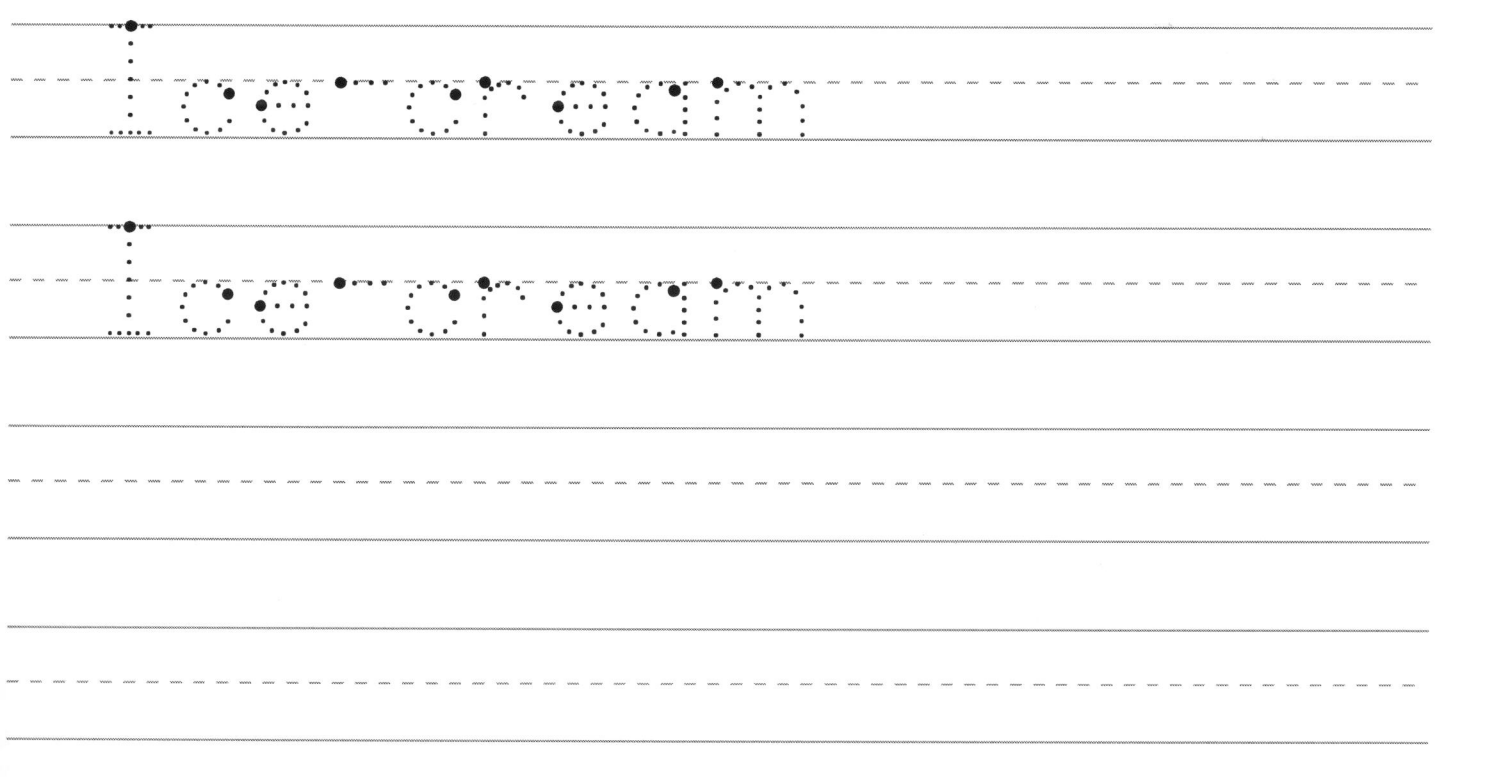

# Ice-cream

Ice-cream

Ice-cream

# Jacket

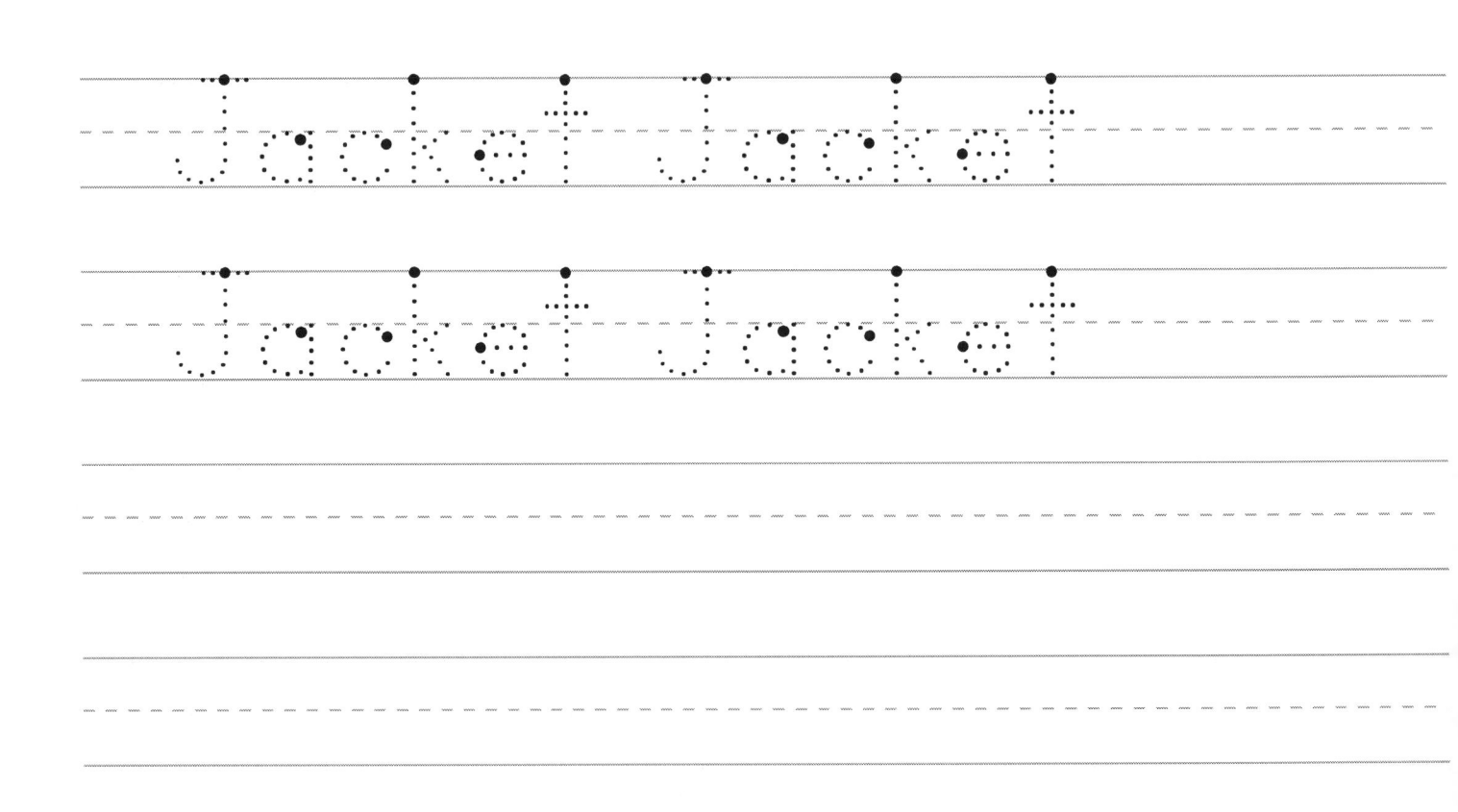

Jacket Jacket

Jacket Jacket

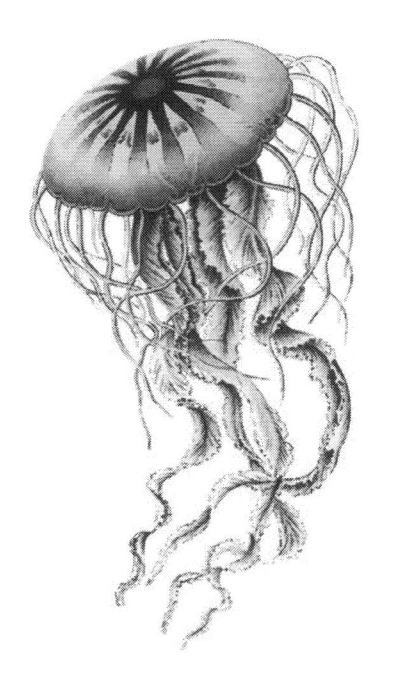

# Jellyfish

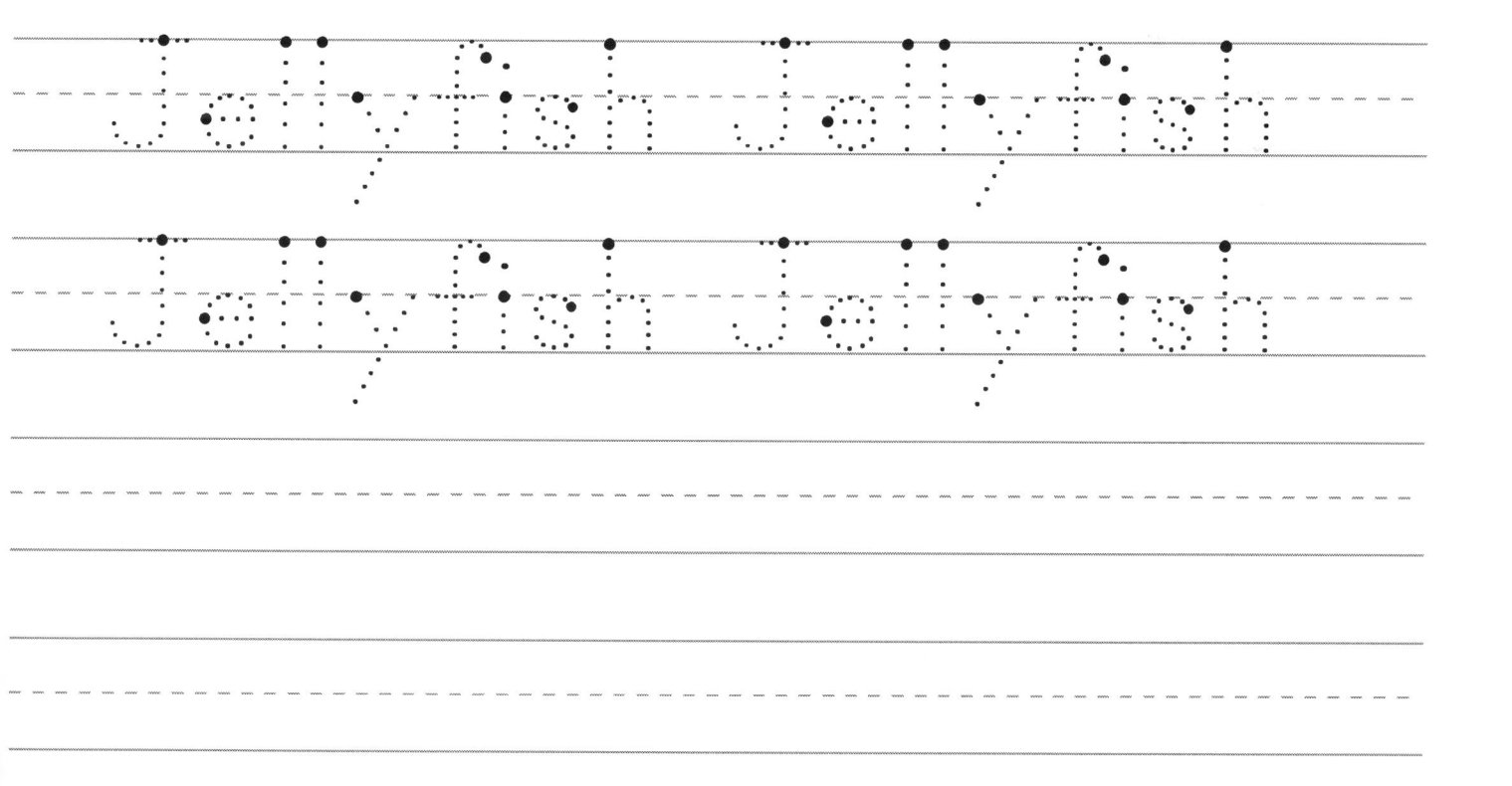

Jellyfish Jellyfish

Jellyfish Jellyfish

# Kangaroo

Kangaroo

Kangaroo

# Koala

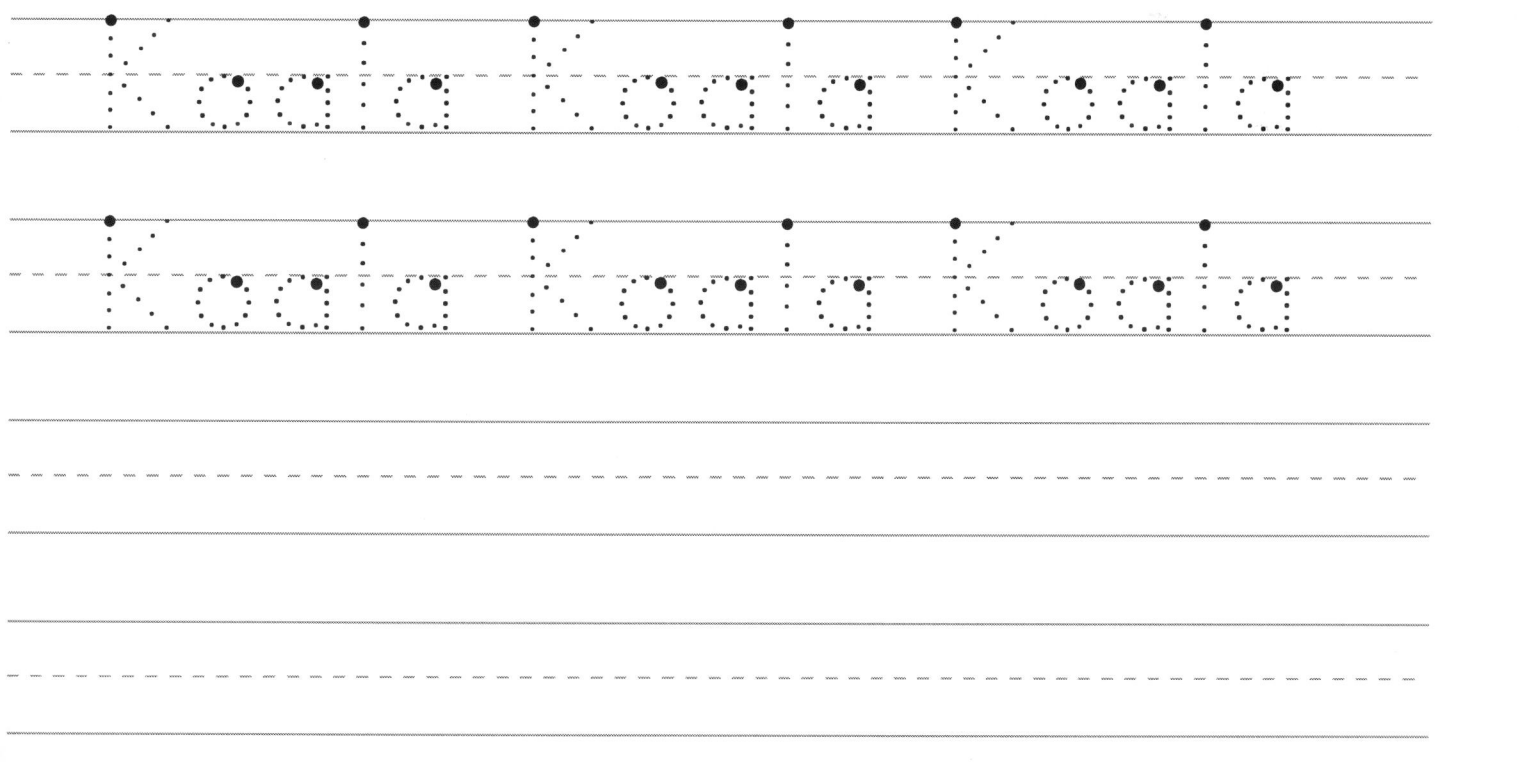

Koala Koala Koala

Koala Koala Koala

# Lion

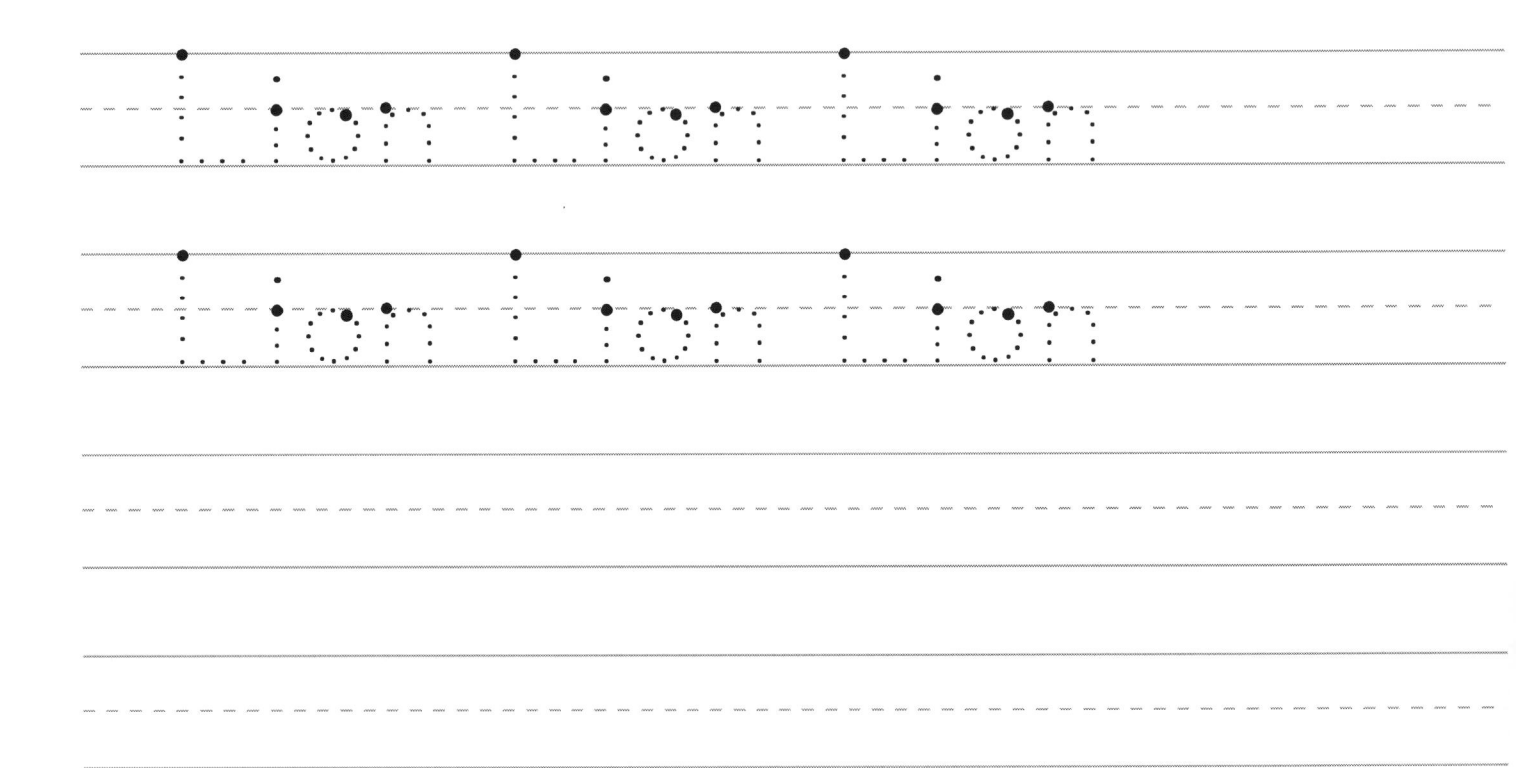

Lion Lion Lion

Lion Lion Lion

# Llama

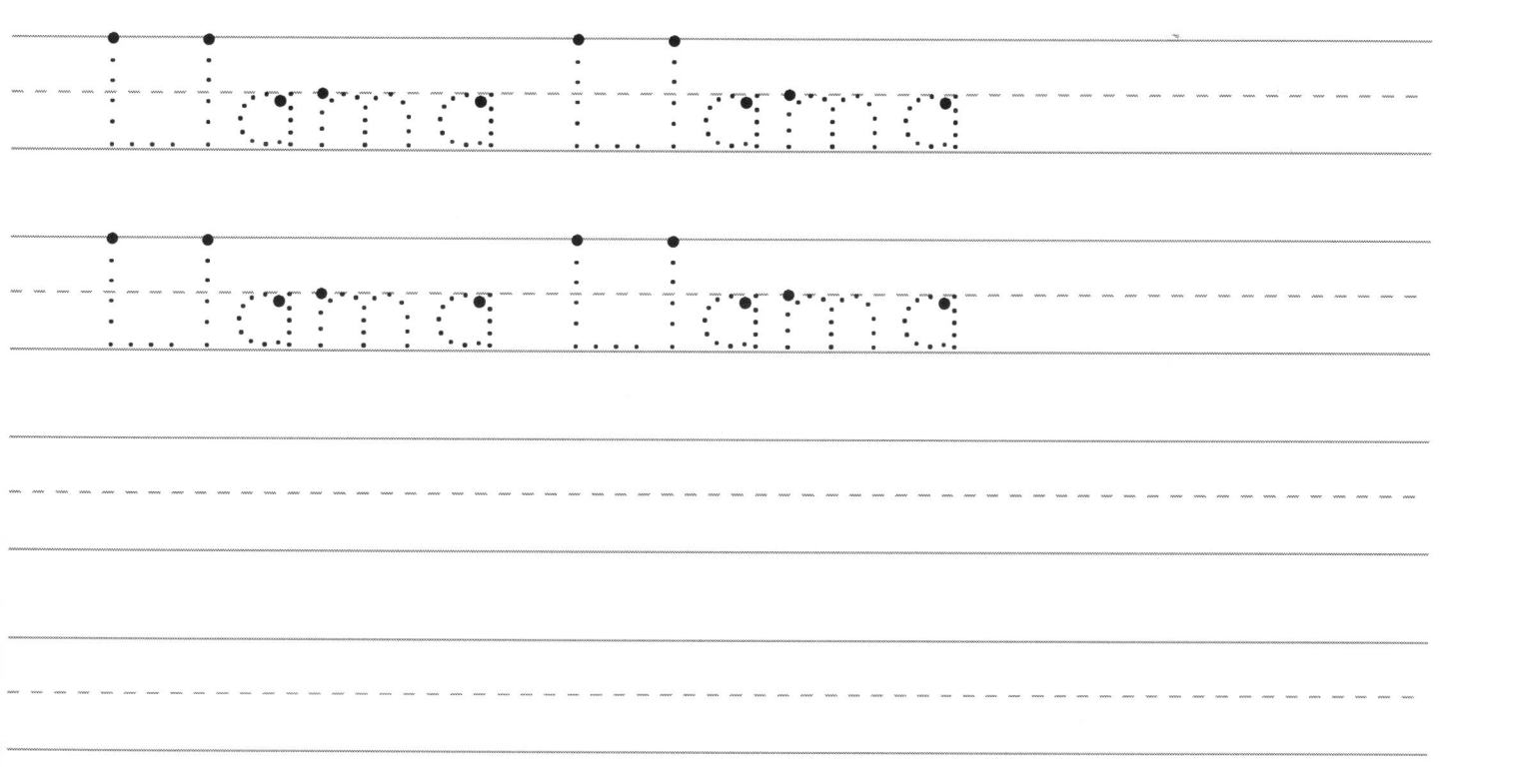

Llama Llama

Llama Llama

# Monkey

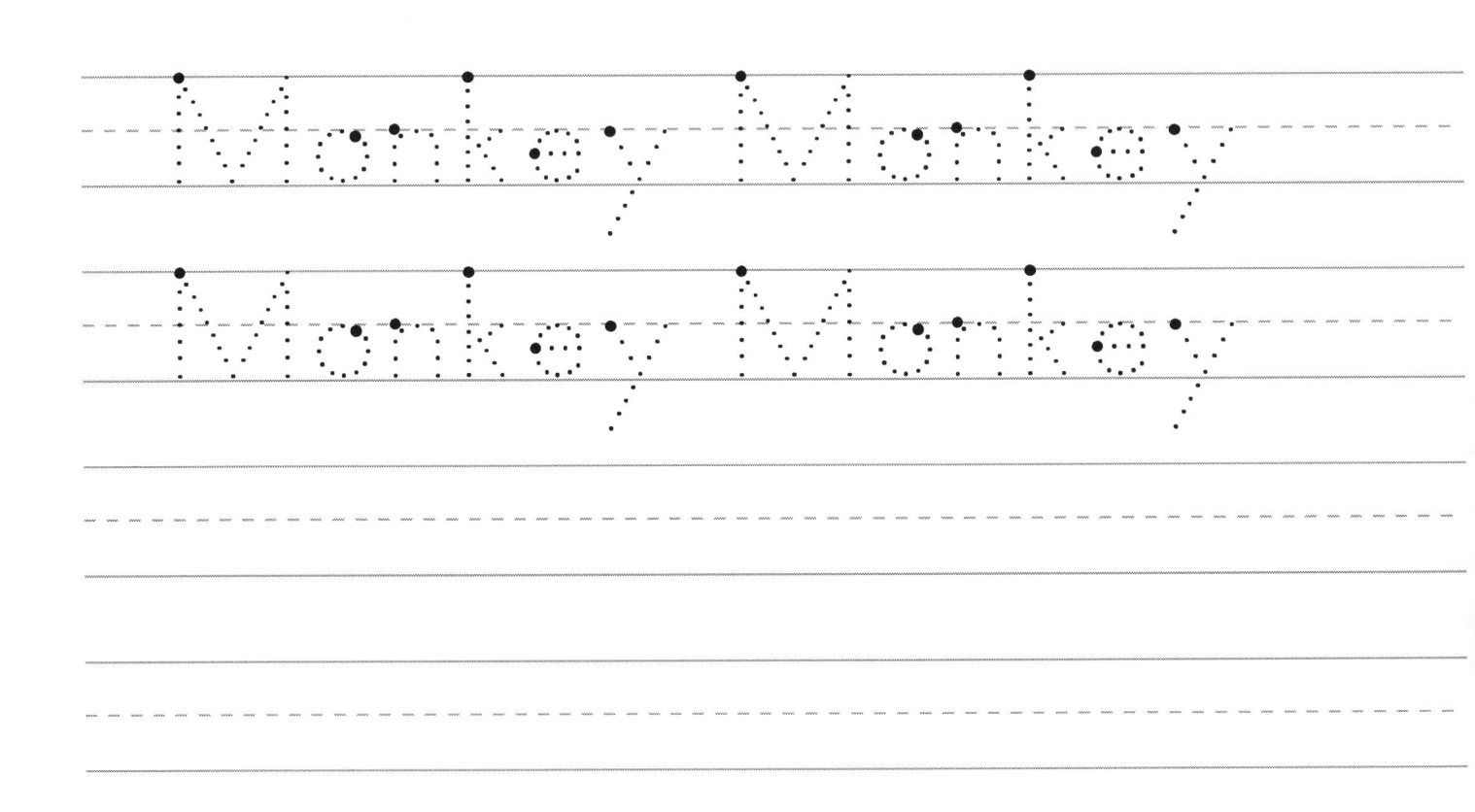

Monkey Monkey

Monkey Monkey

# Money

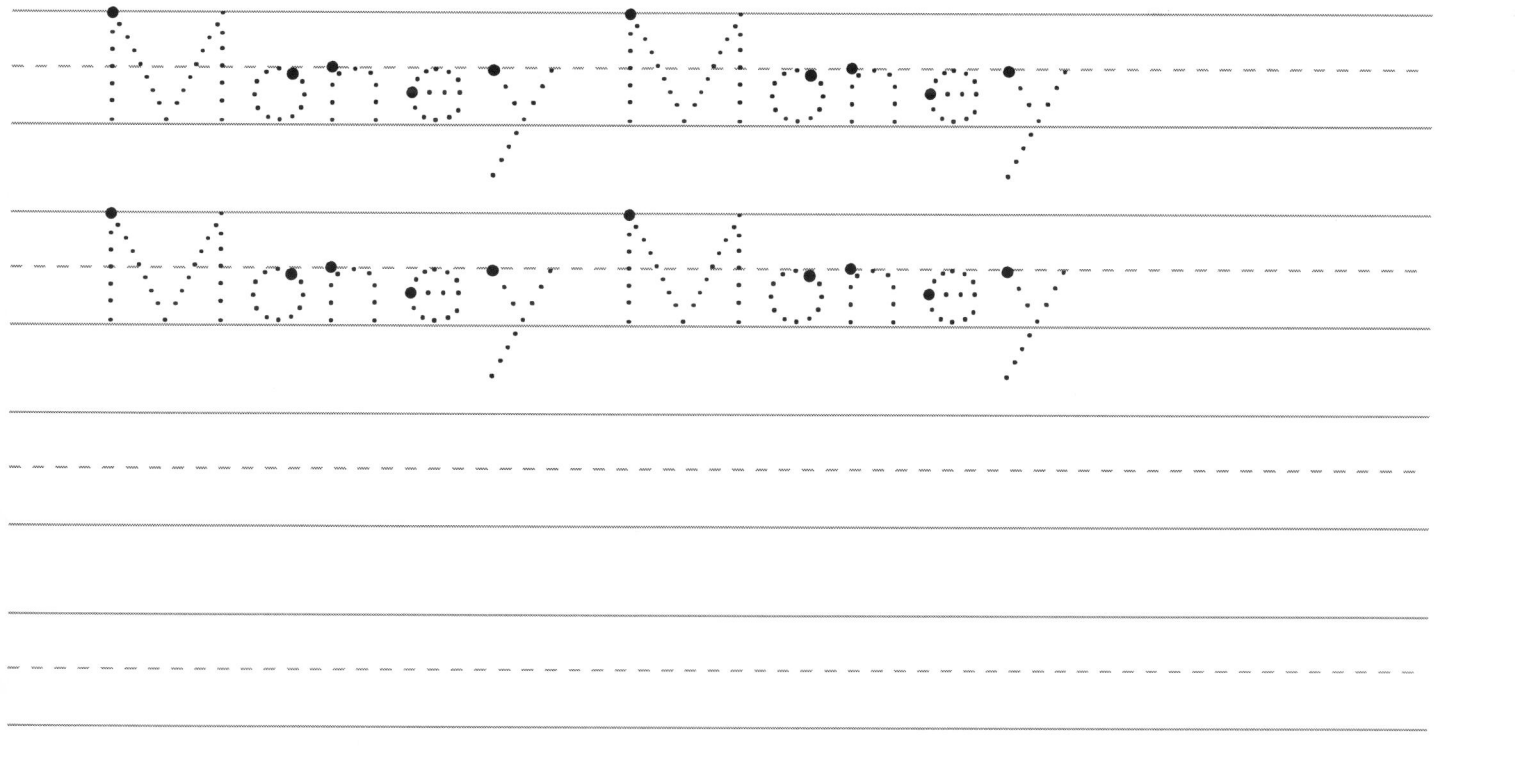

Money Money
Money Money

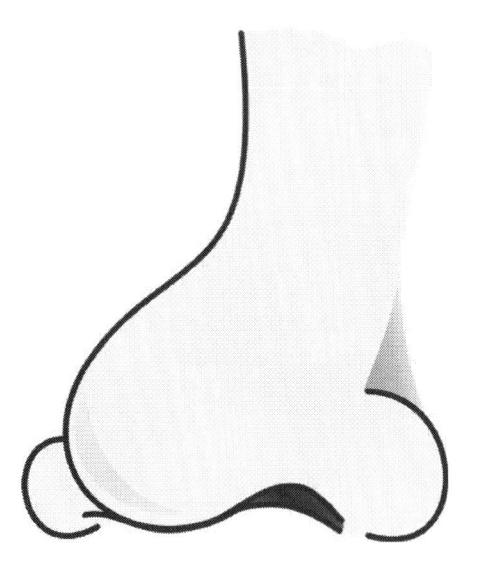

# Nose

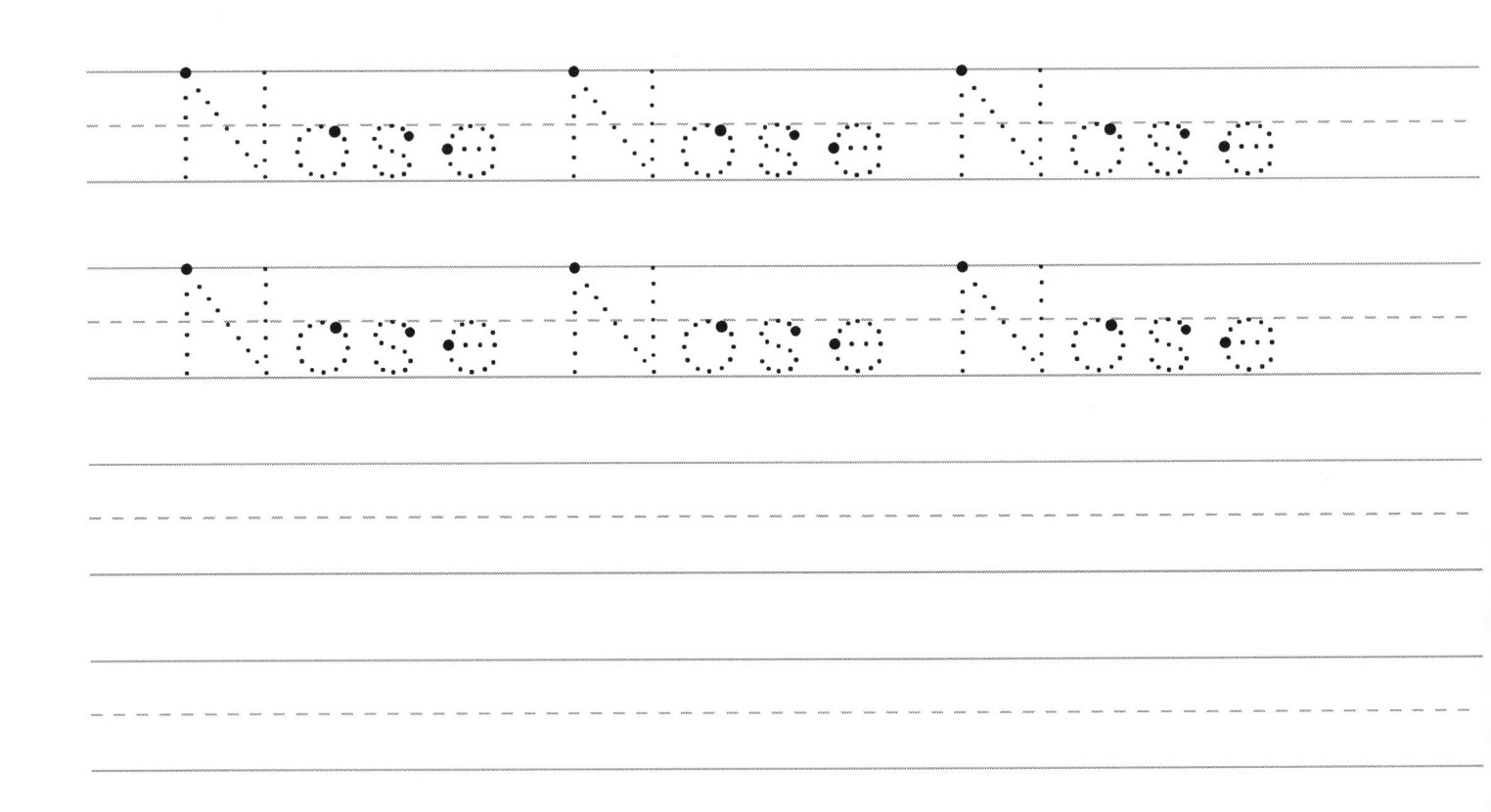

Nose Nose Nose

Nose Nose Nose

# Number

0 1 2 3 4
5 6 7 8 9

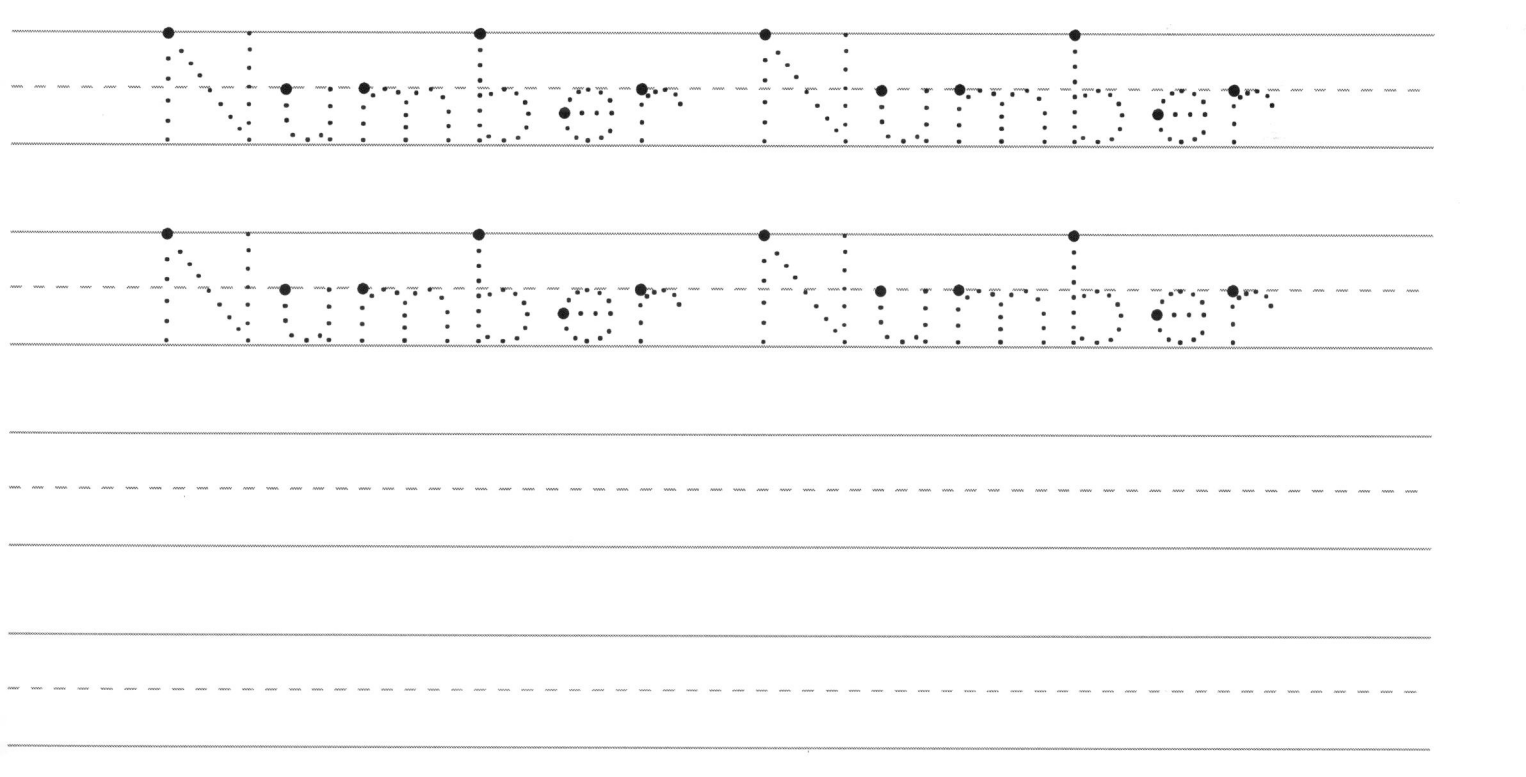

Number Number

Number Number

# Orange

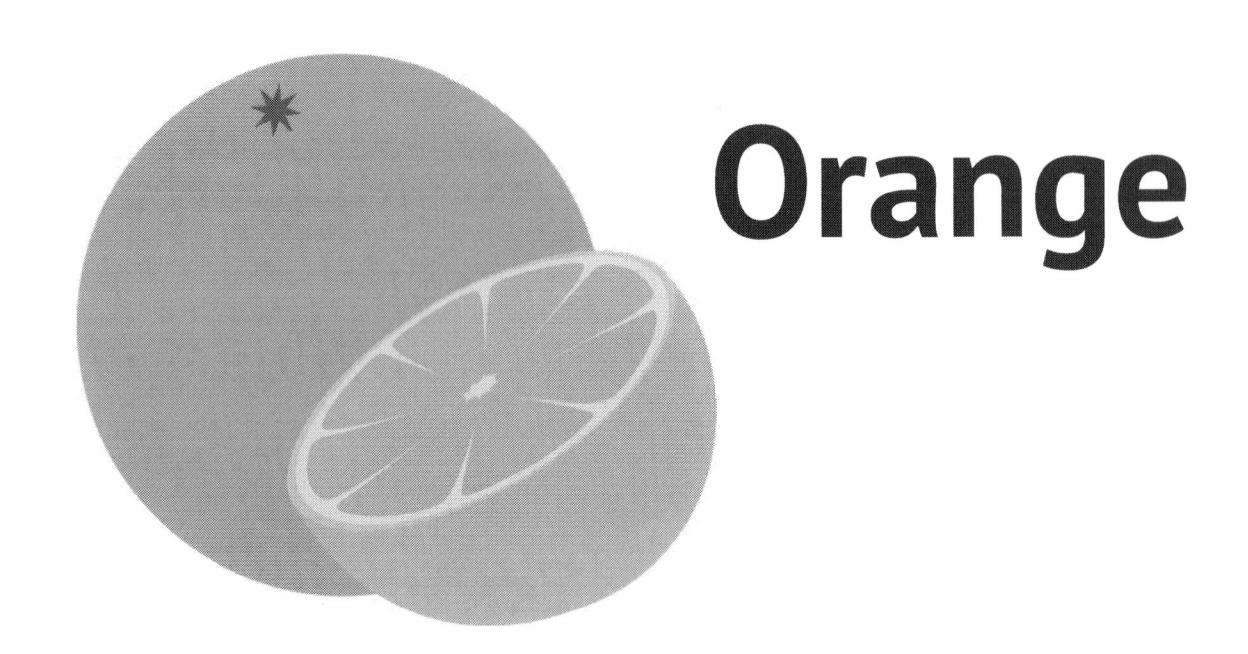

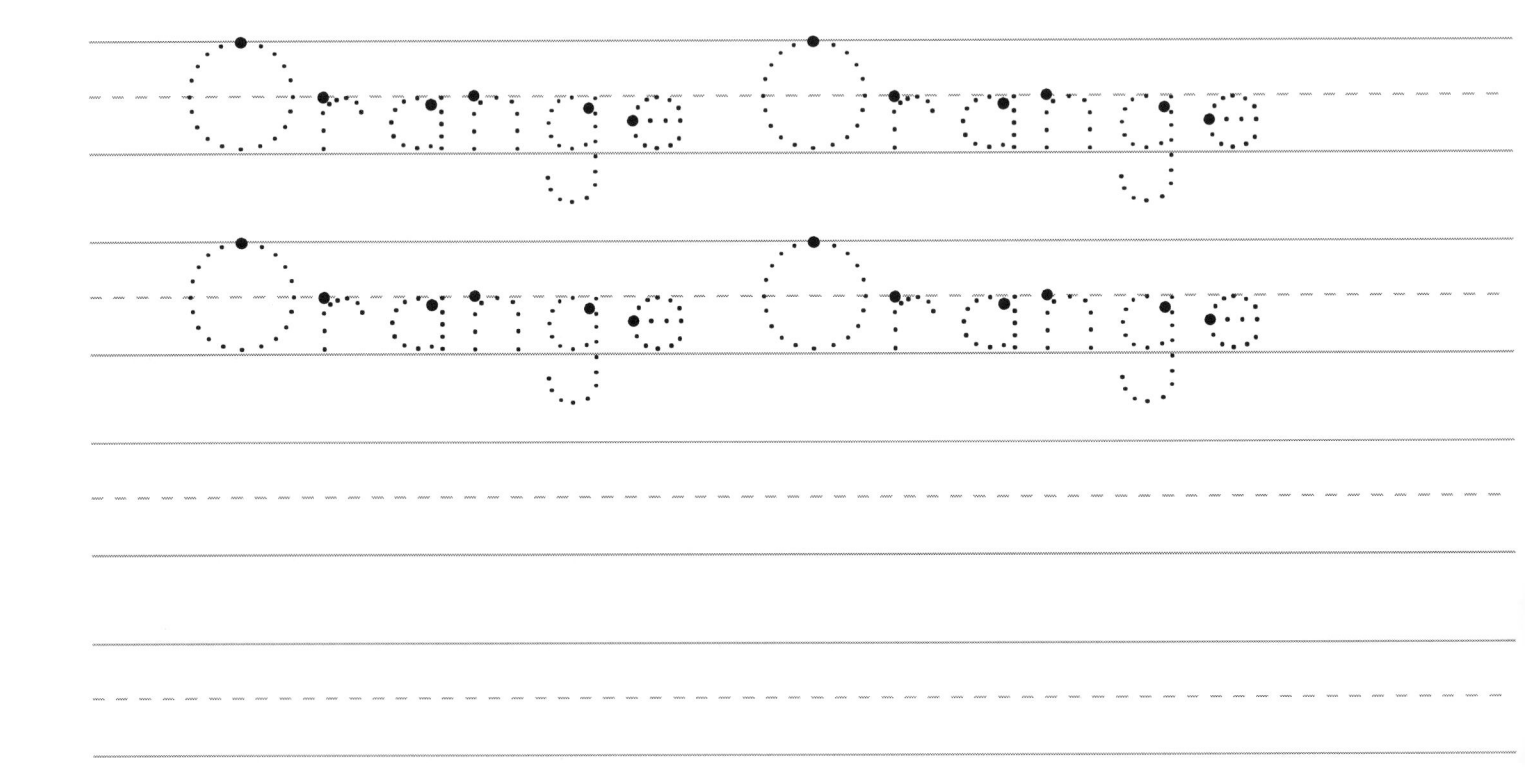

Orange Orange

Orange Orange

# Octopus

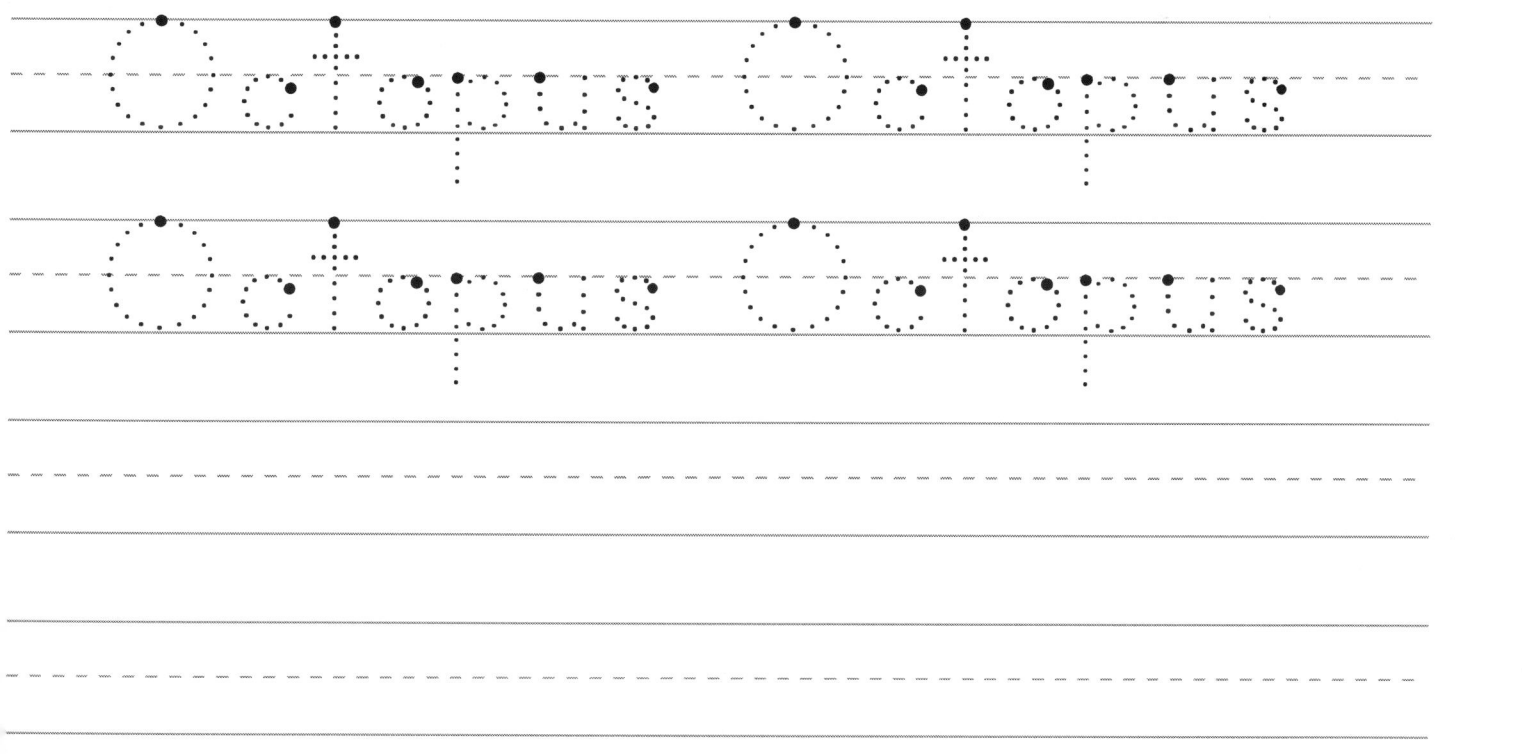

Octopus Octopus

Octopus Octopus

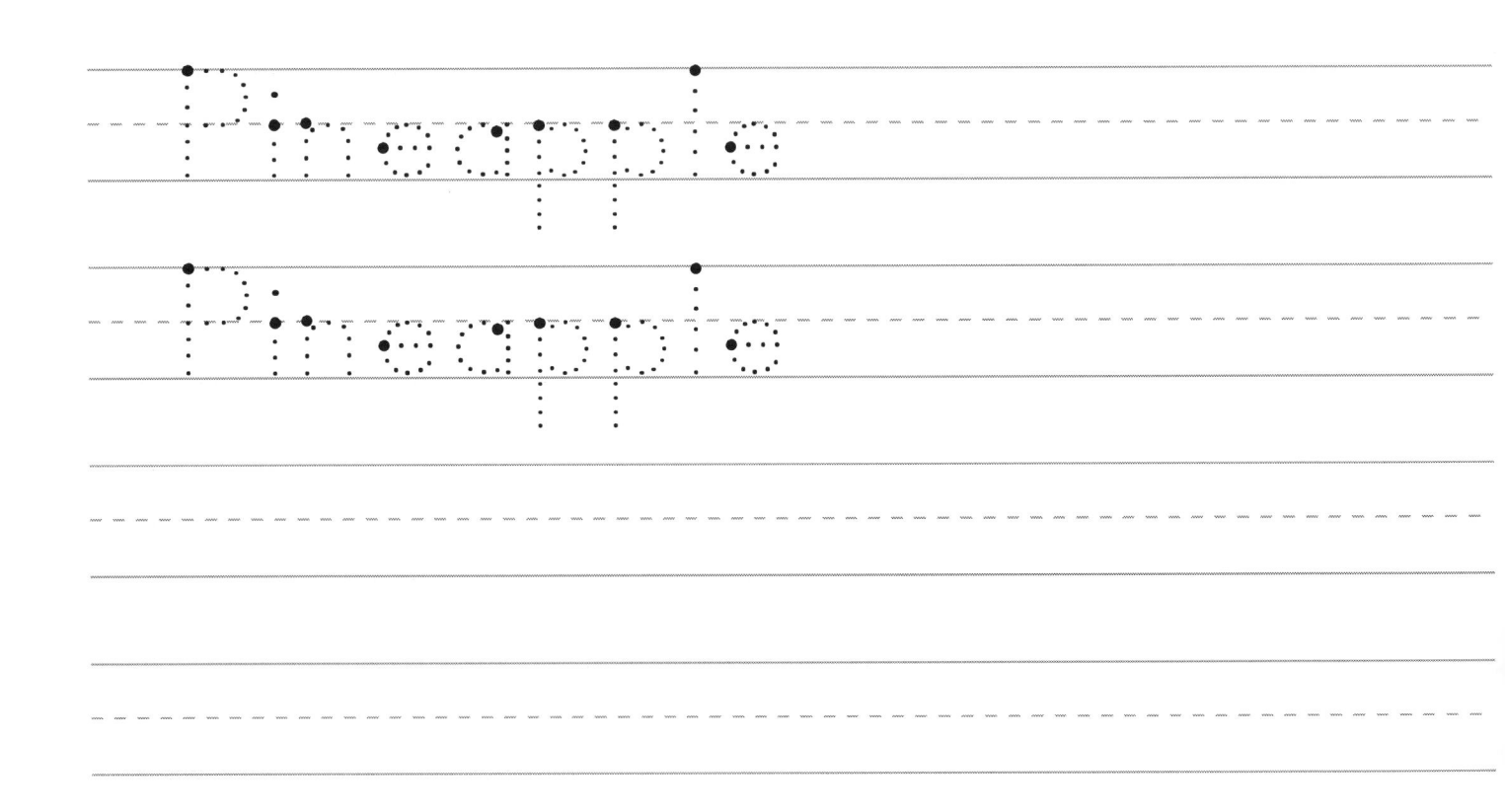

# Pineapple

Pineapple

Pineapple

# Pirate

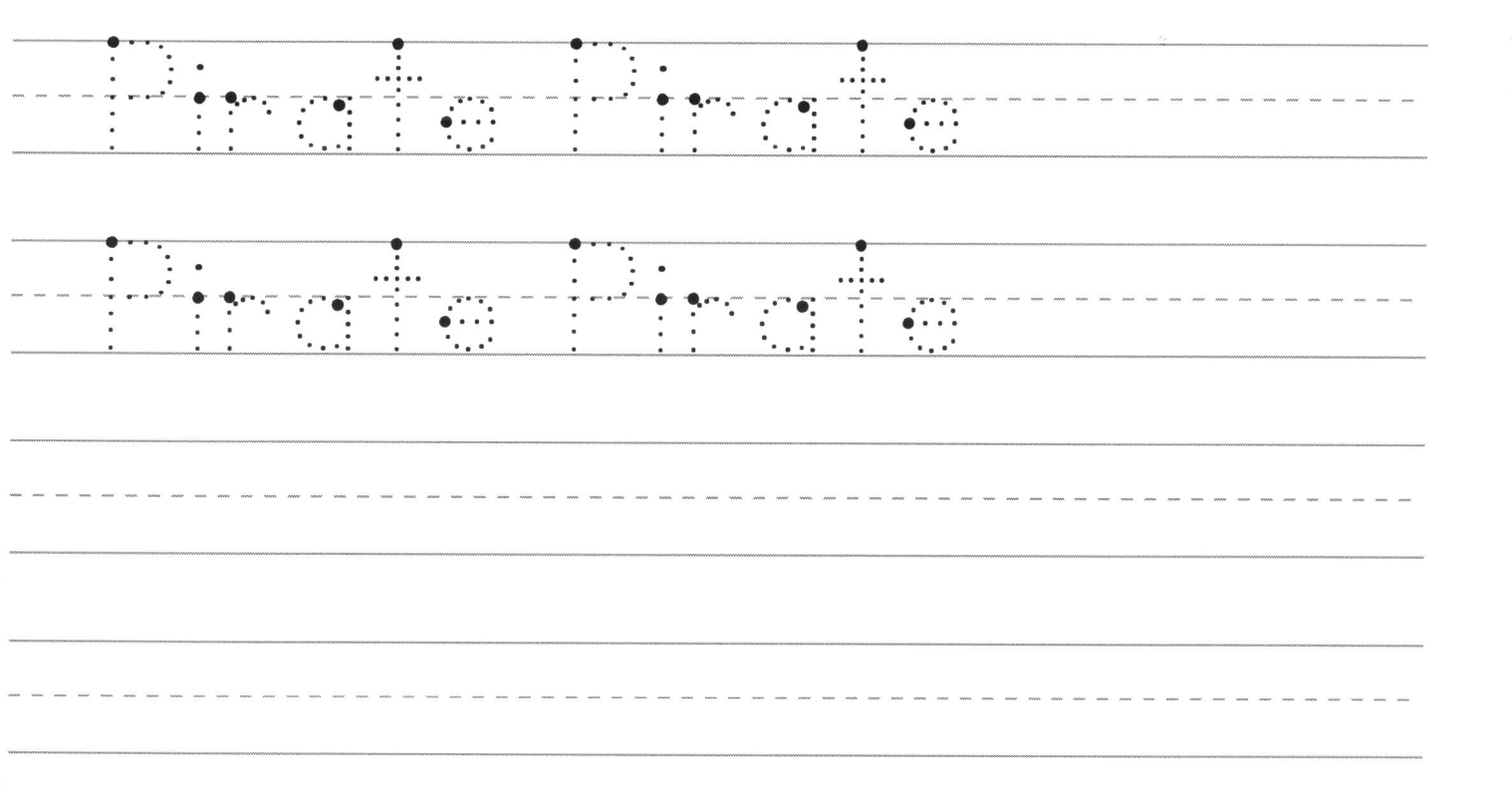

Pirate Pirate

Pirate Pirate

# Queen

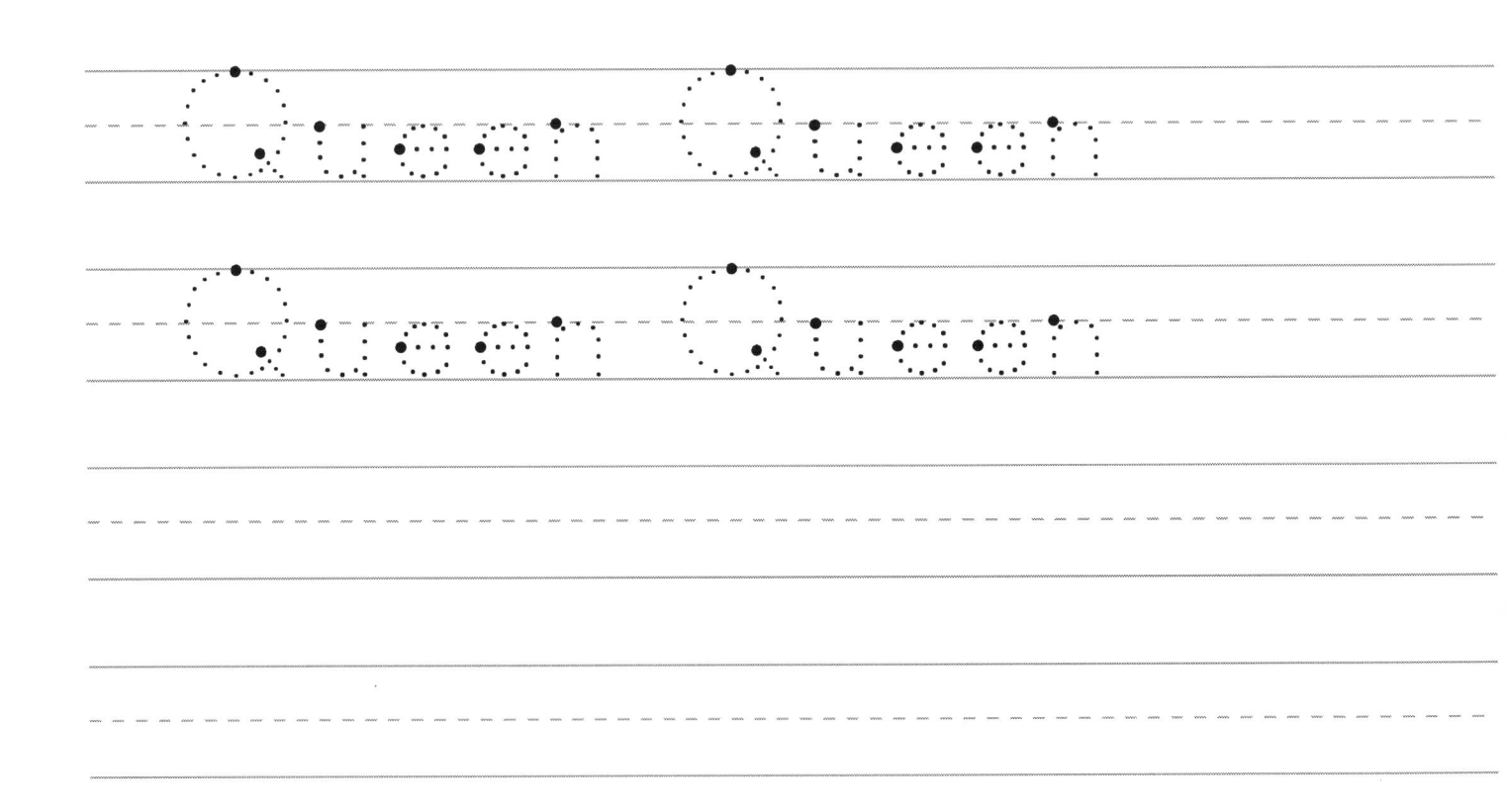

Queen Queen

Queen Queen

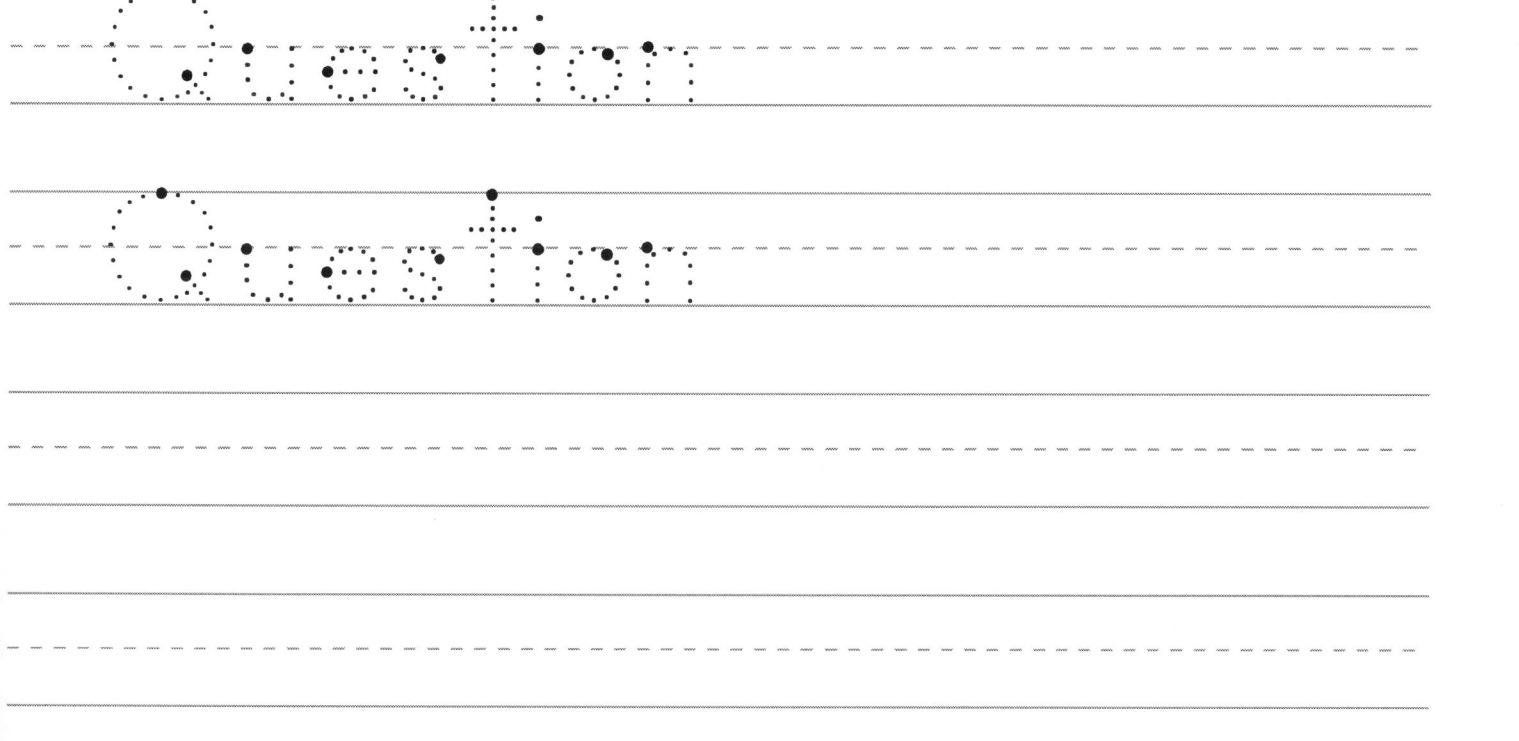

# ? Question

Question

Question

# Rainbow

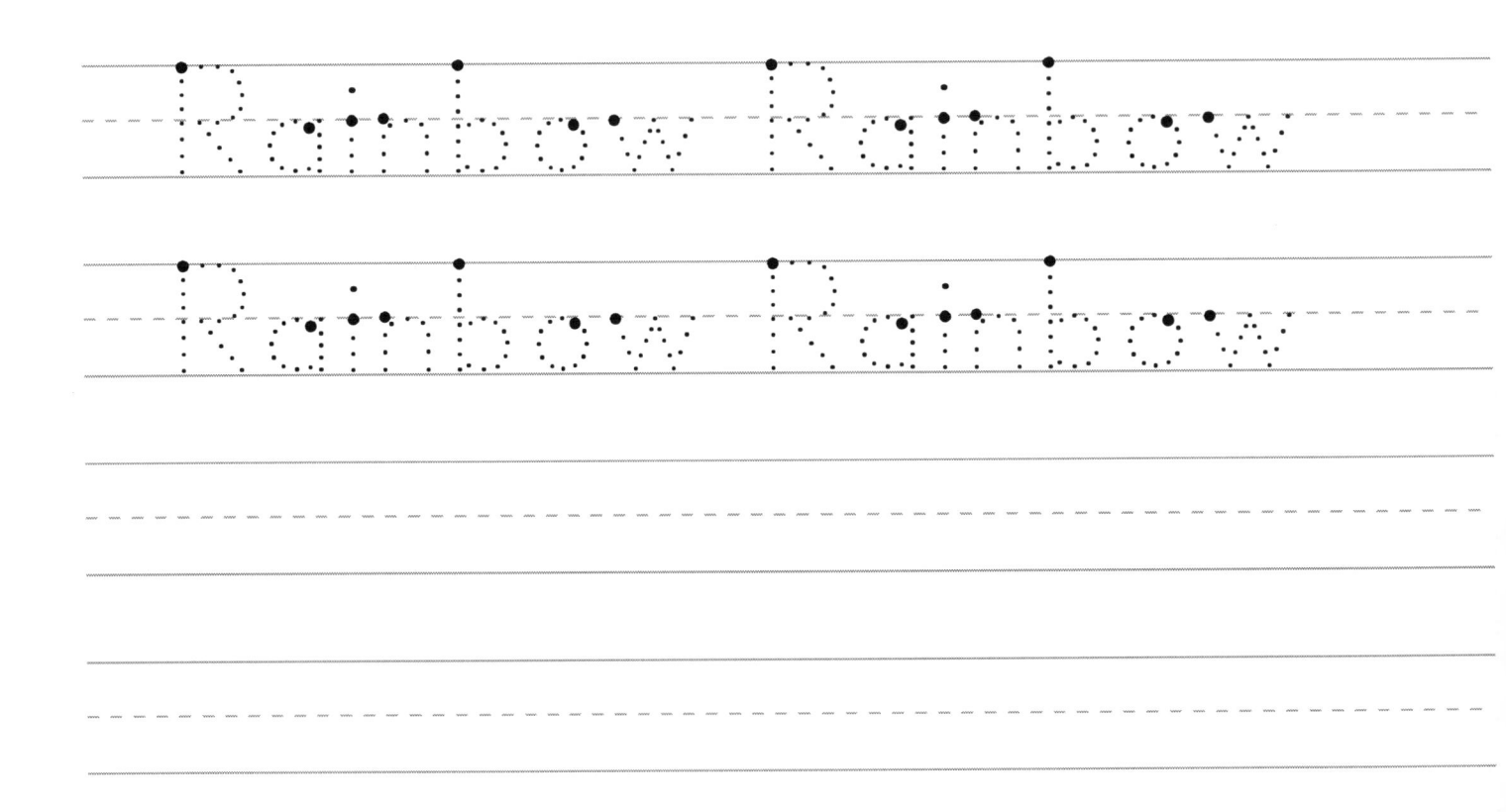

Rainbow Rainbow

Rainbow Rainbow

# Rat

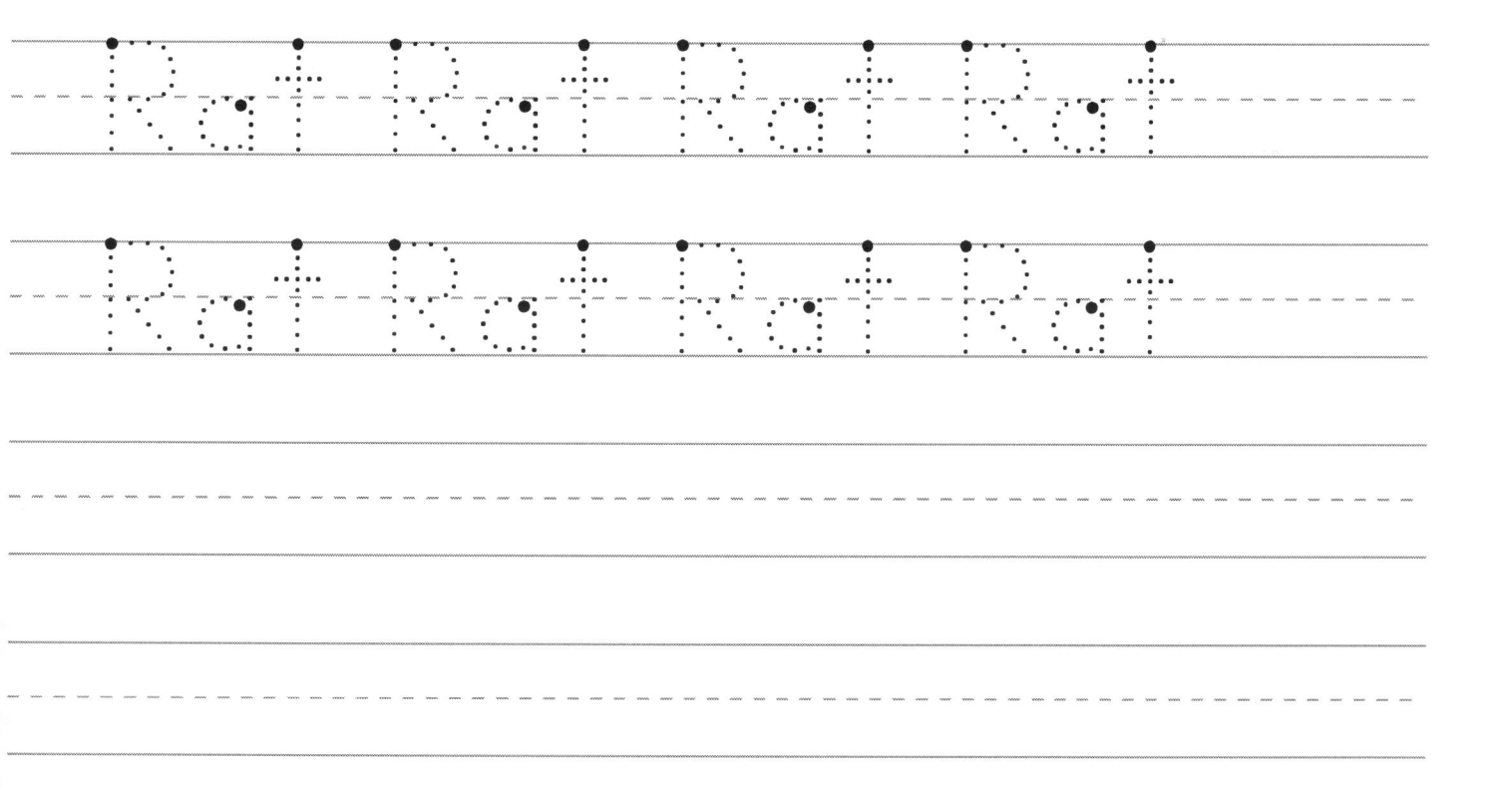

Rat Rat Rat Rat

Rat Rat Rat Rat

# Snake

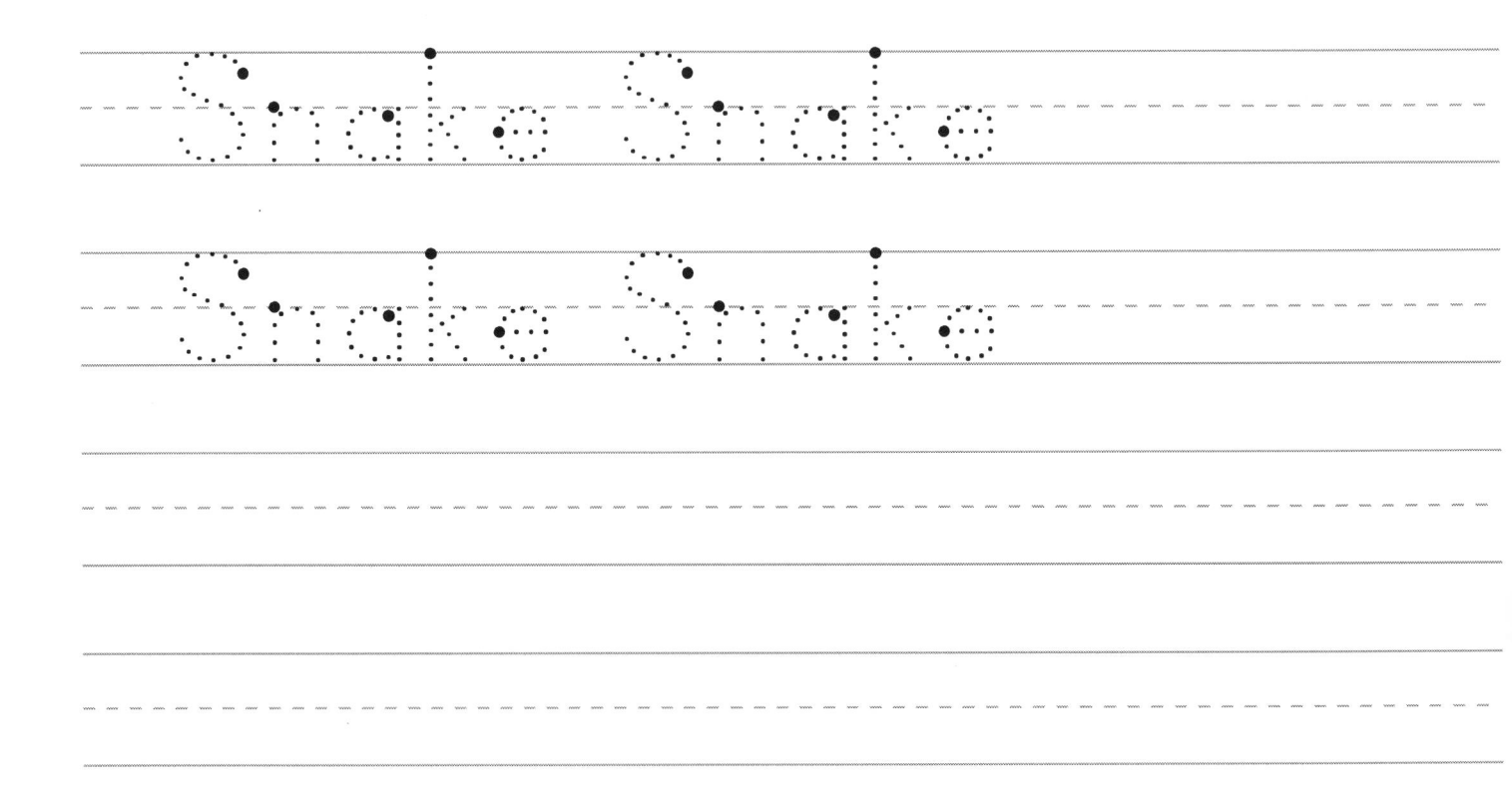

Snake Snake

Snake Snake

# Squirrel

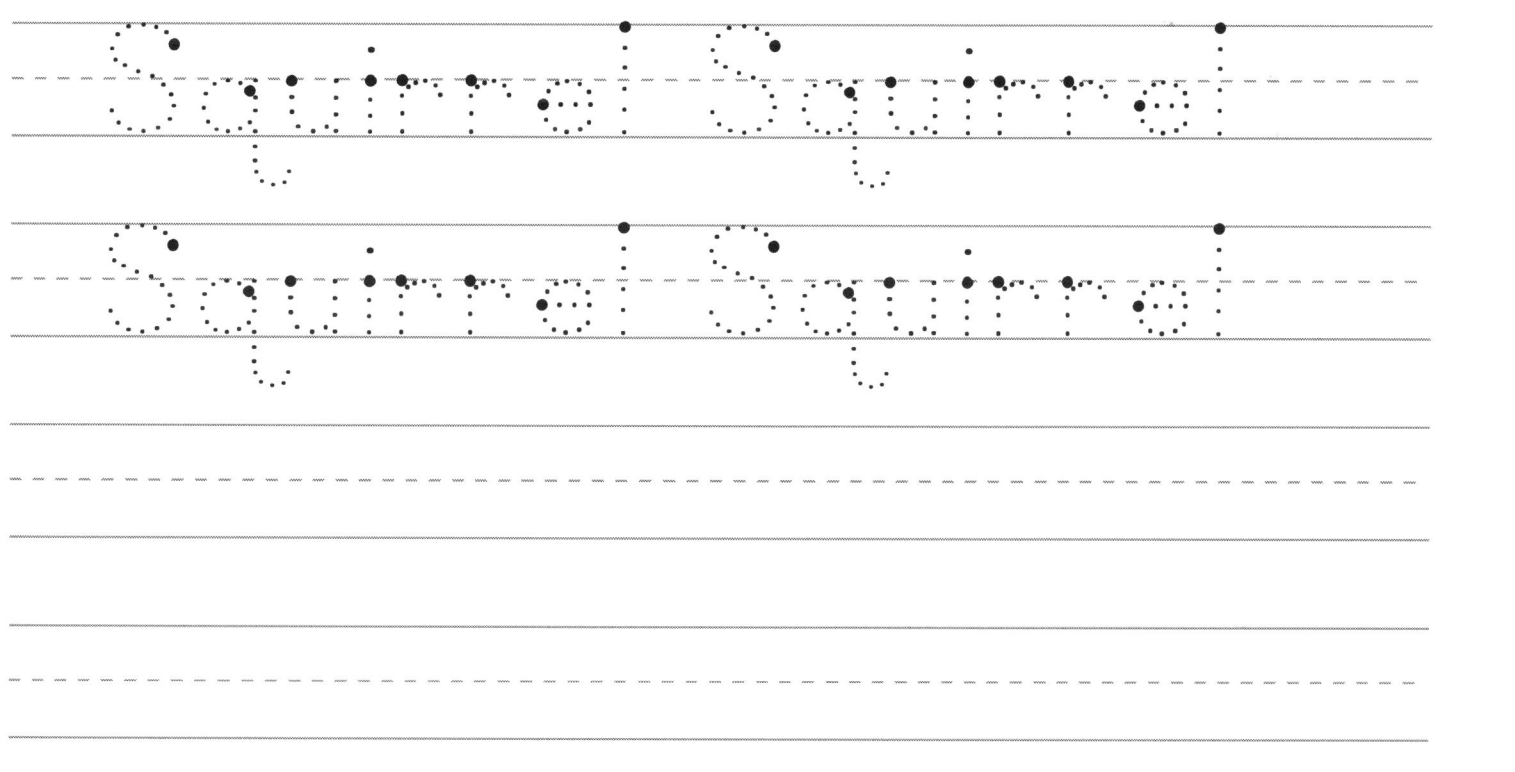

Squirrel Squirrel

Squirrel Squirrel

# Tortoise

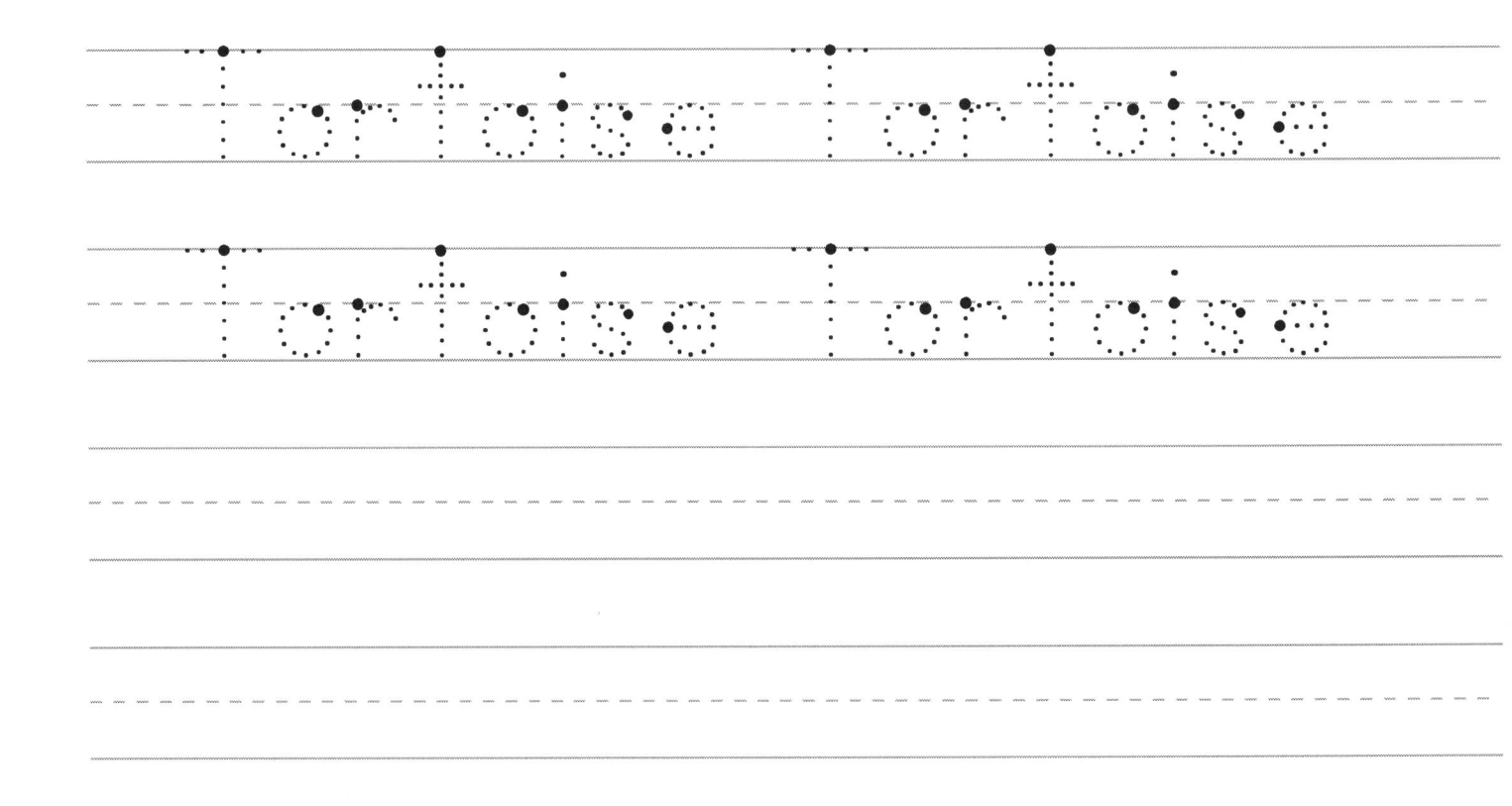

Tortoise Tortoise

Tortoise Tortoise

# Tiger

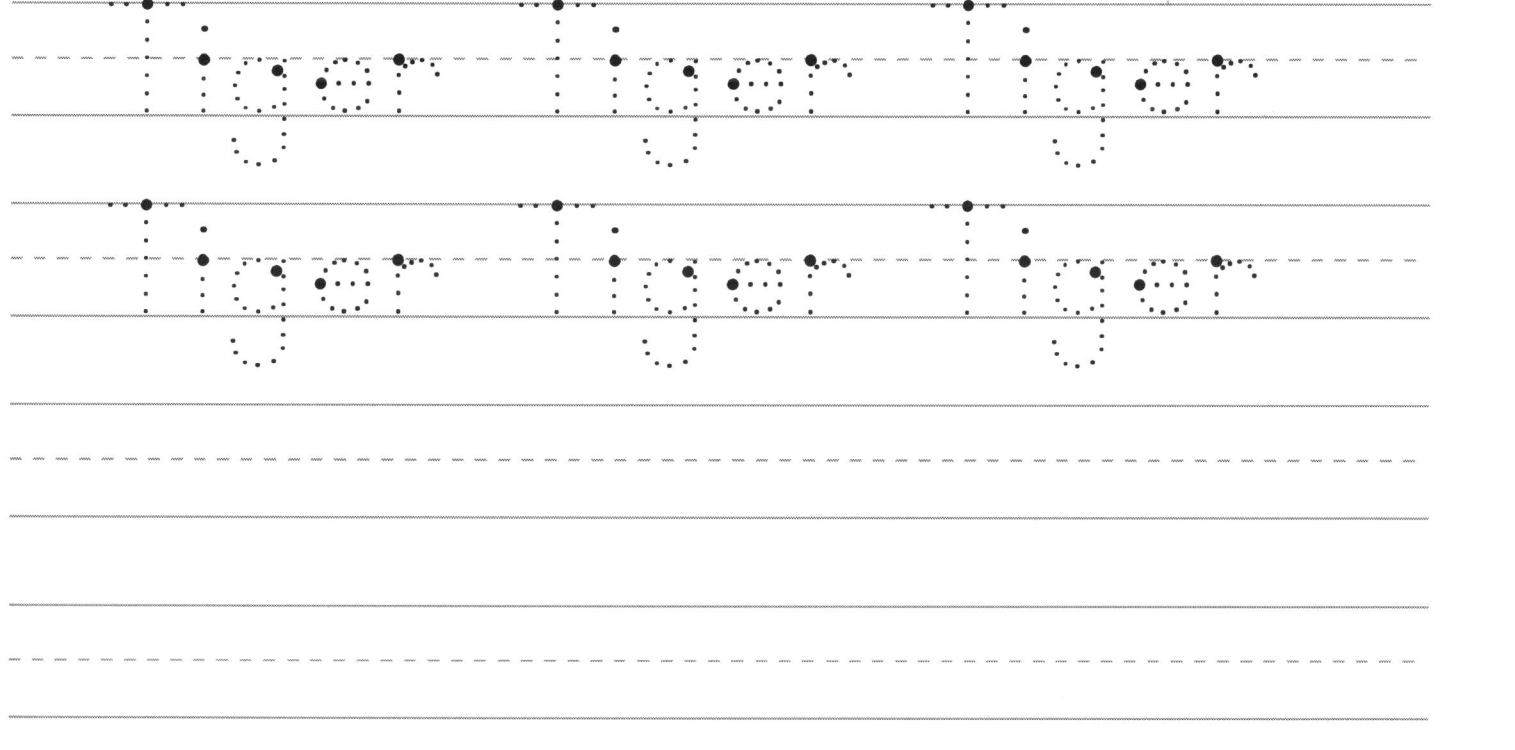

Tiger Tiger Tiger

Tiger Tiger Tiger

# Umbrella

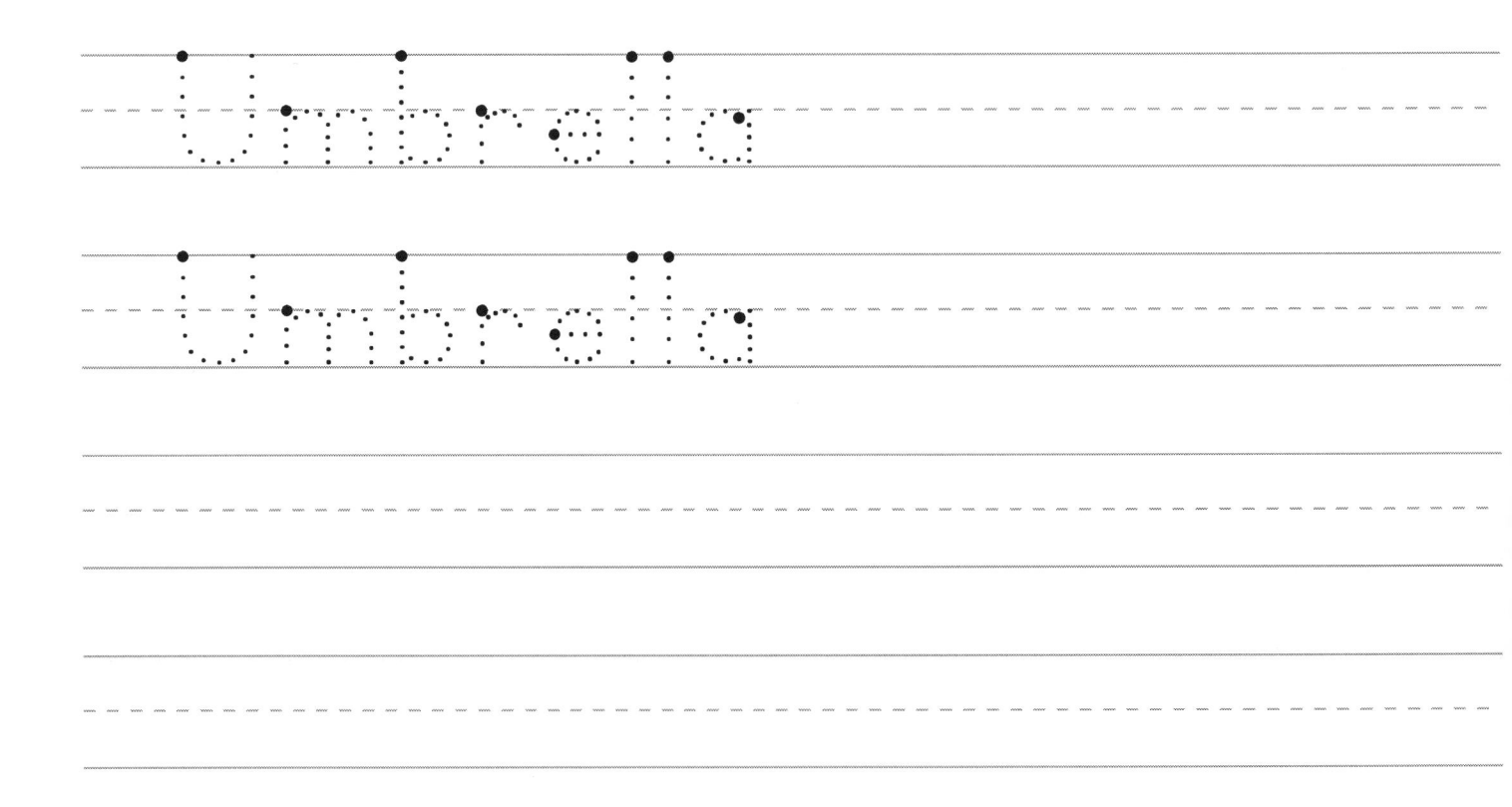

Umbrella

Umbrella

# UFO

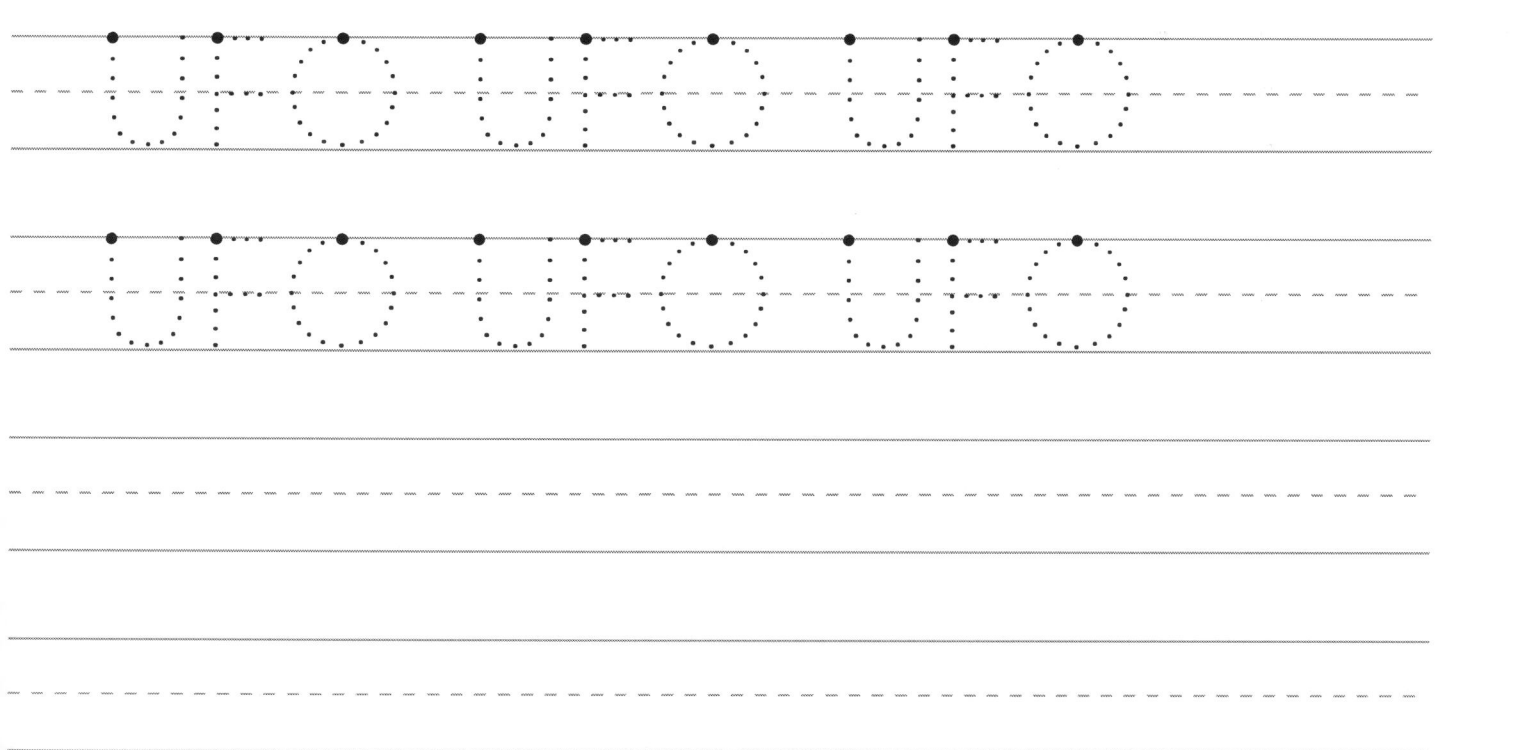

UFO UFO UFO

UFO UFO UFO

# Vulture

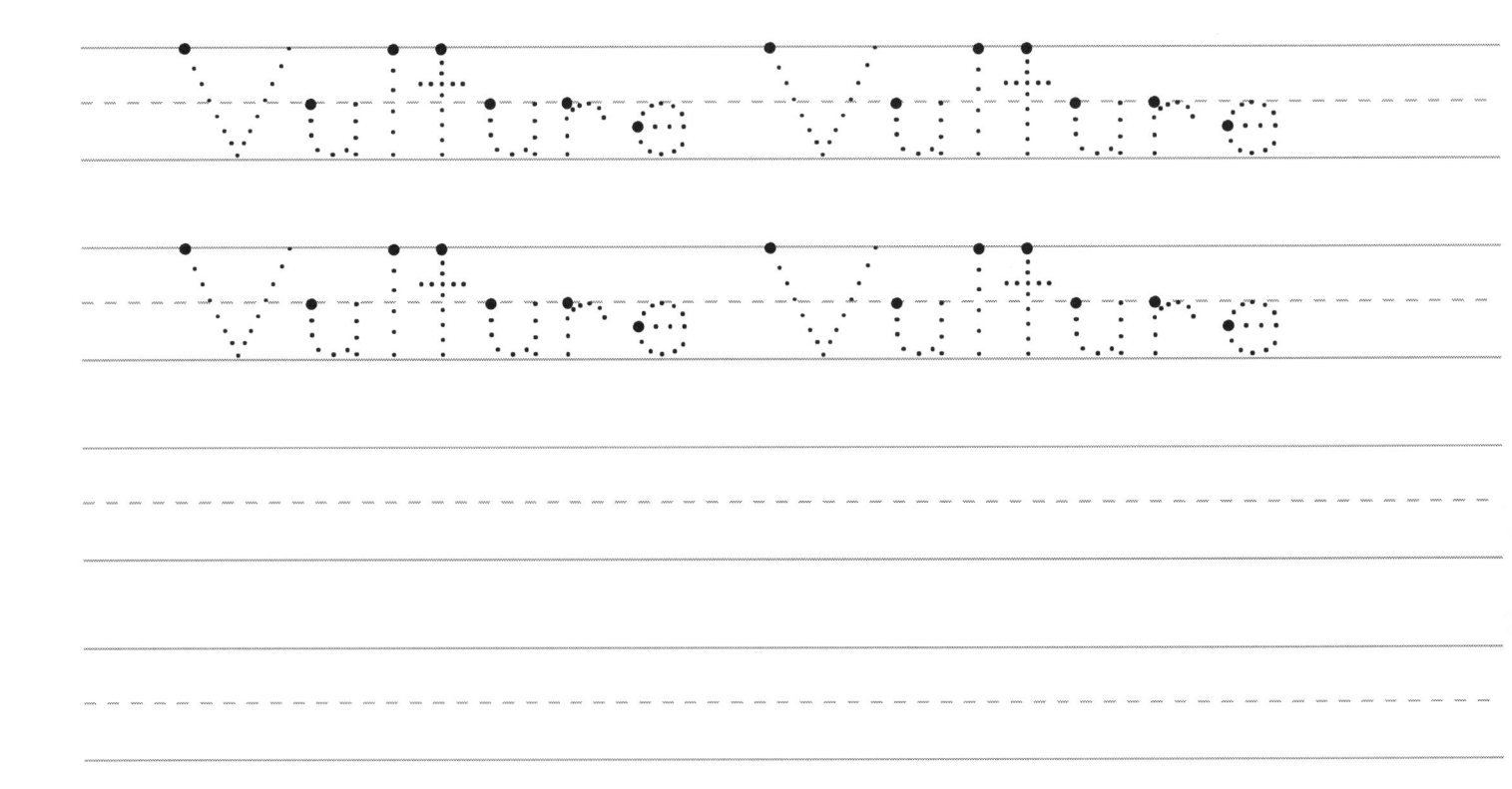

Vulture Vulture

Vulture Vulture

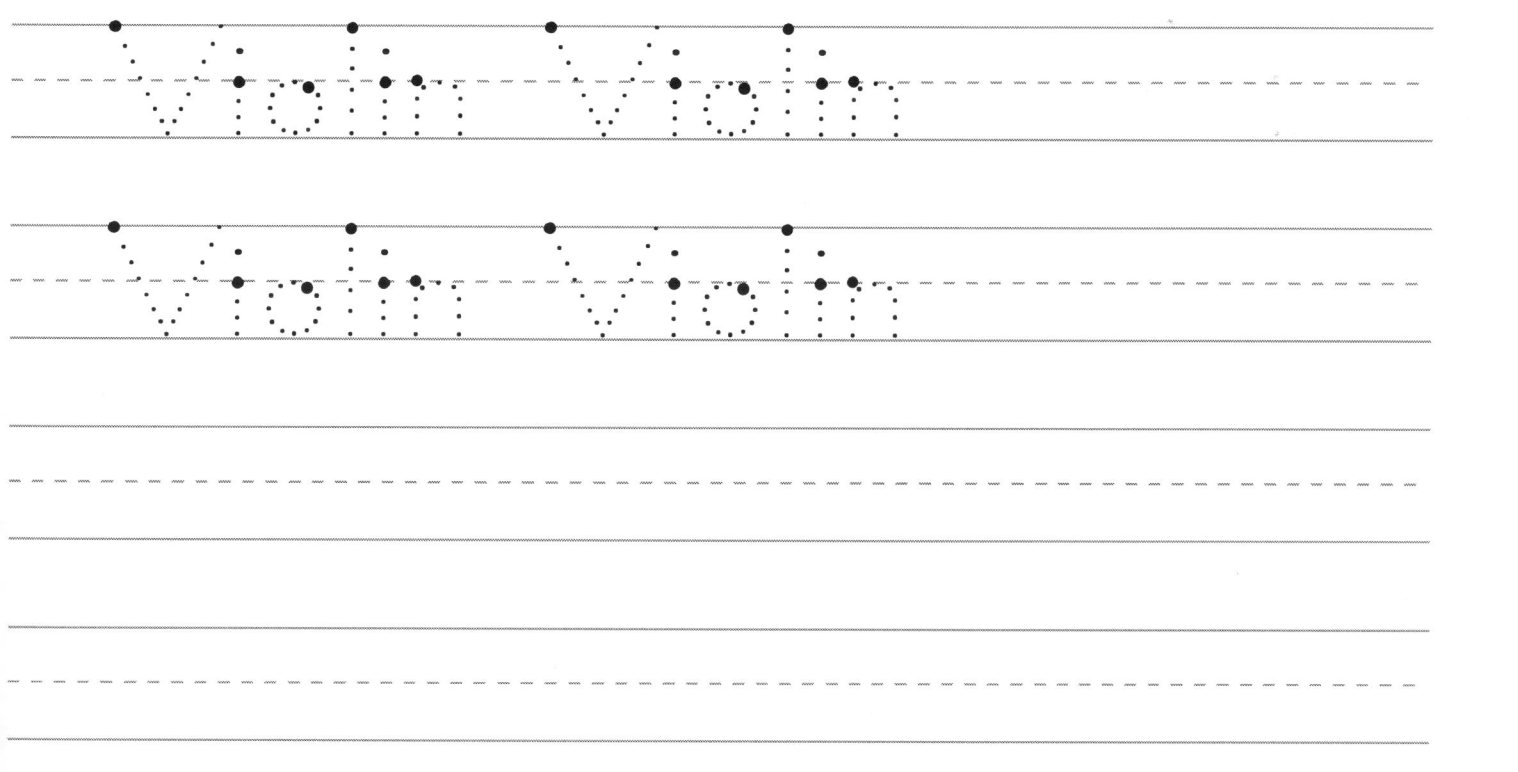

# Violin

Violin Violin

Violin Violin

# Whale

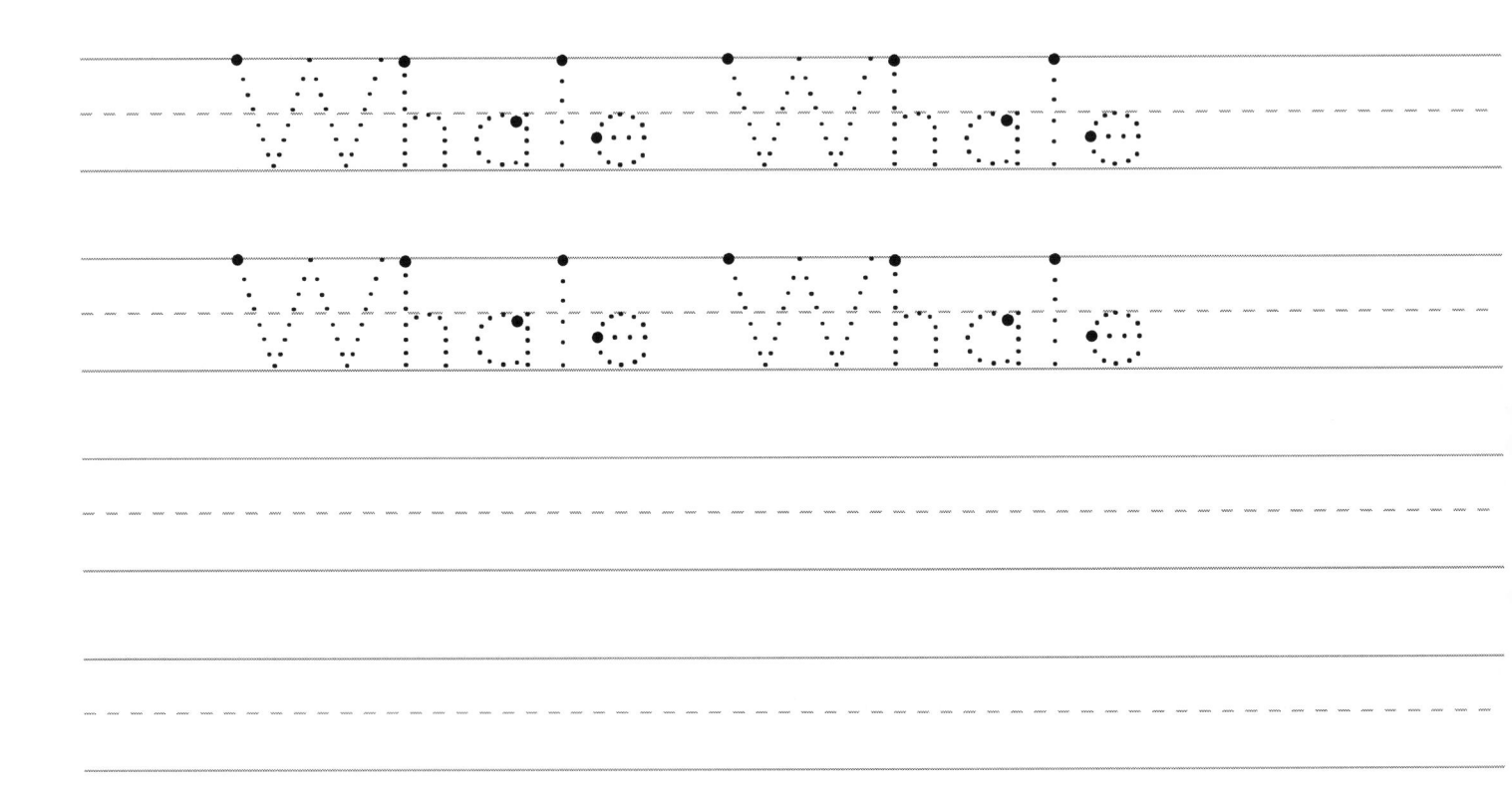

Whale Whale

Whale Whale

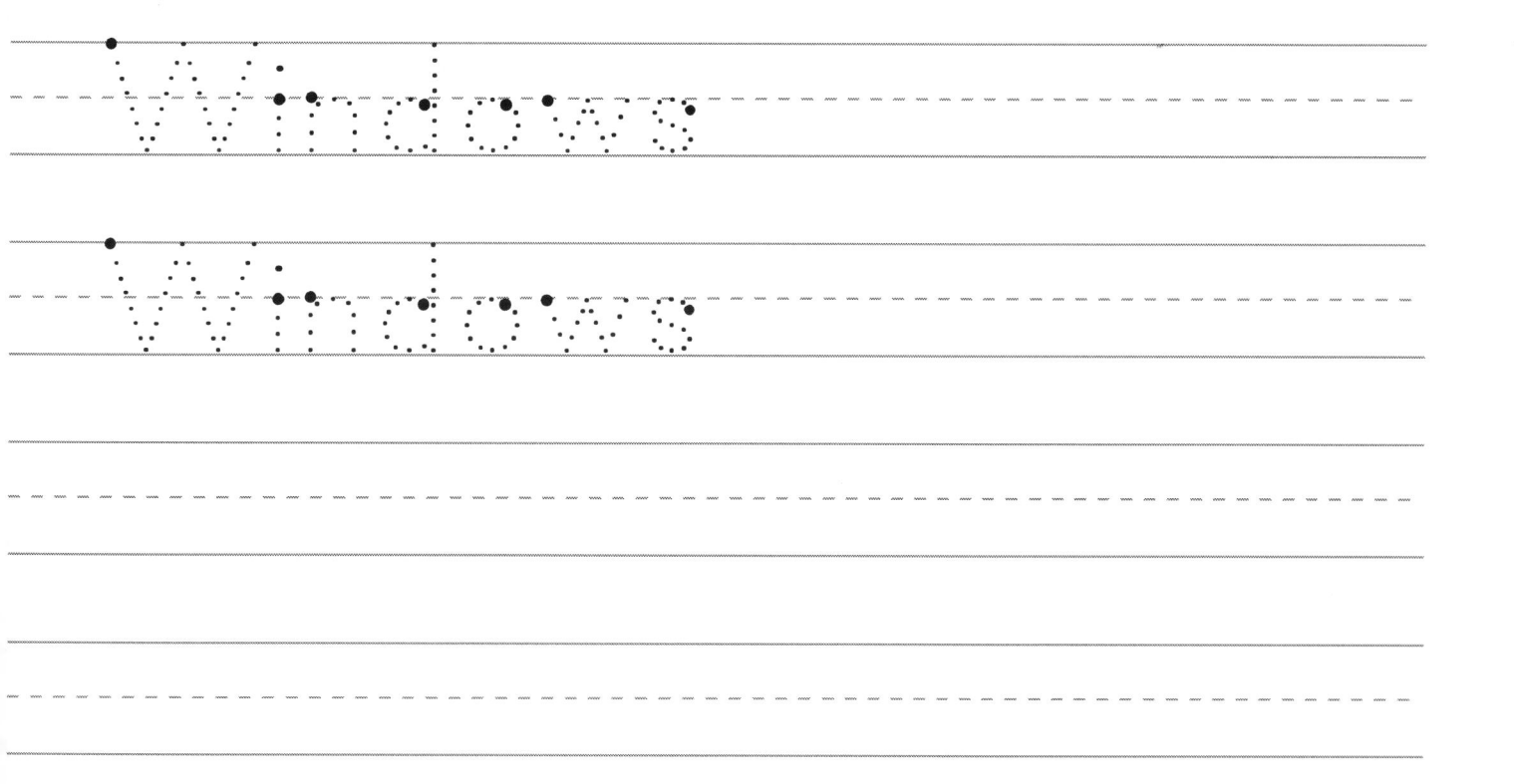

# Windows

Windows

Windows

# Xmas

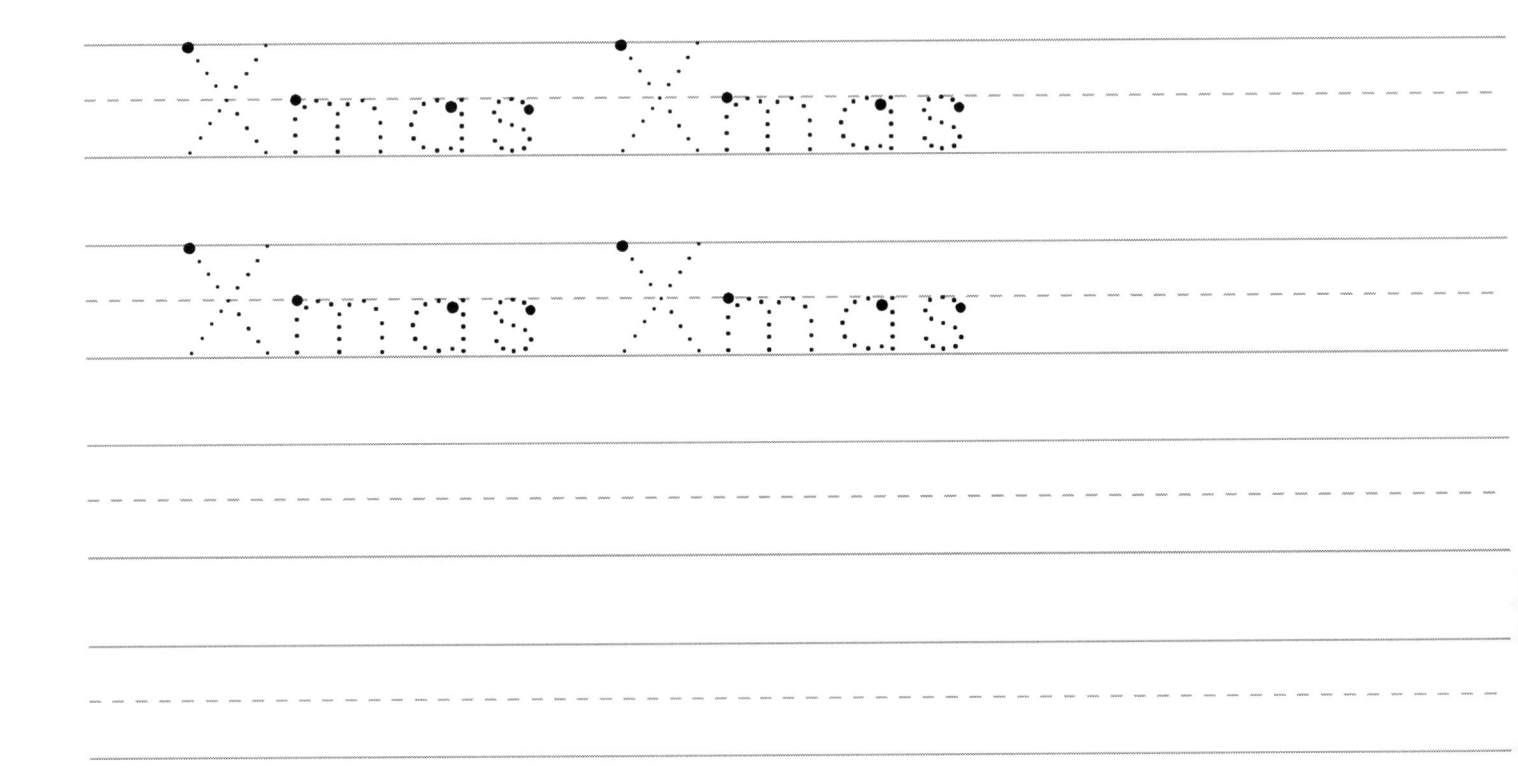

Xmas Xmas

Xmas Xmas

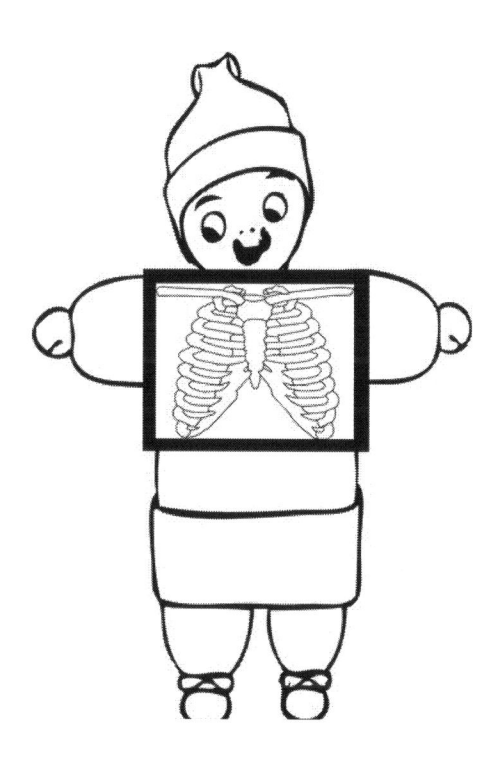

# X-ray

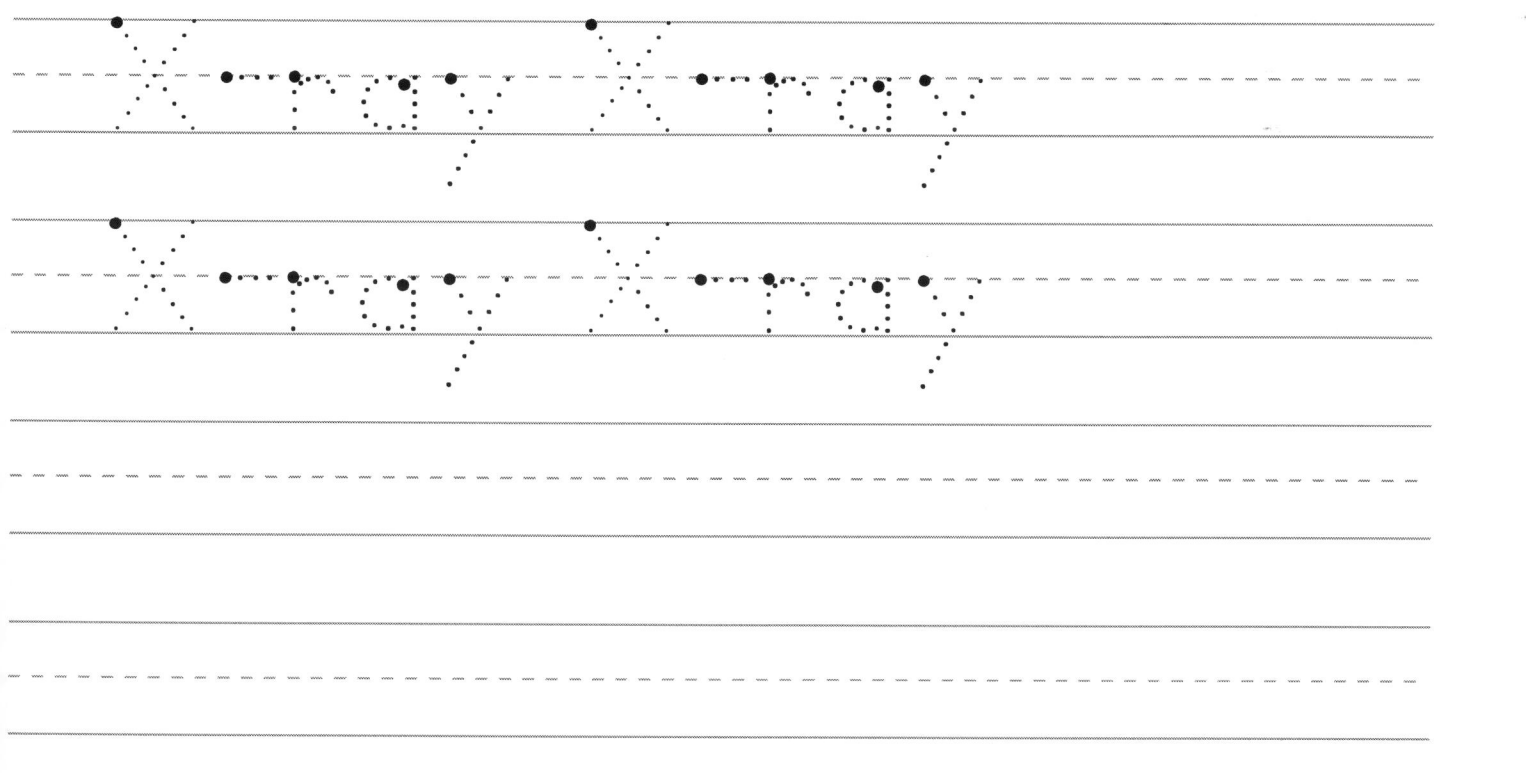

X-ray X-ray
X-ray X-ray

# Yacht

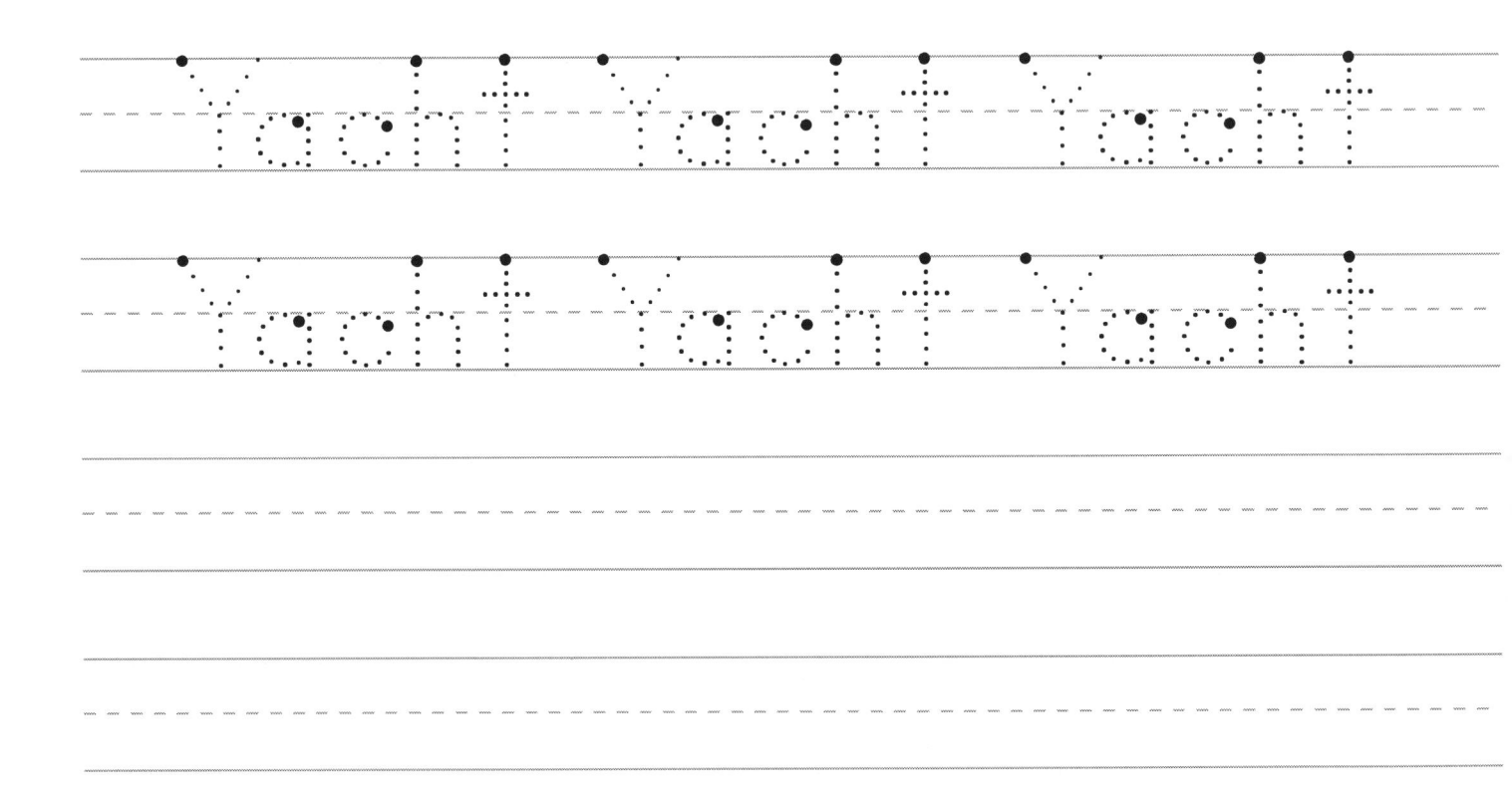

Yacht Yacht Yacht

Yacht Yacht Yacht

# Yarn

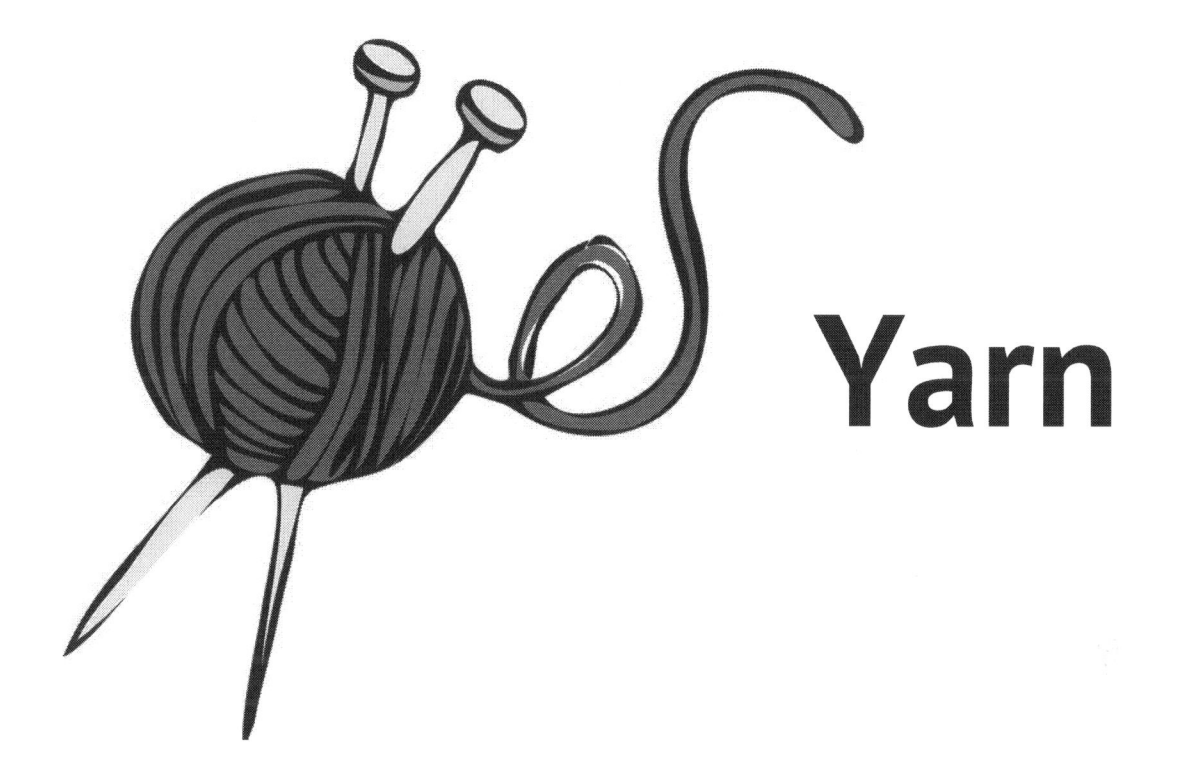

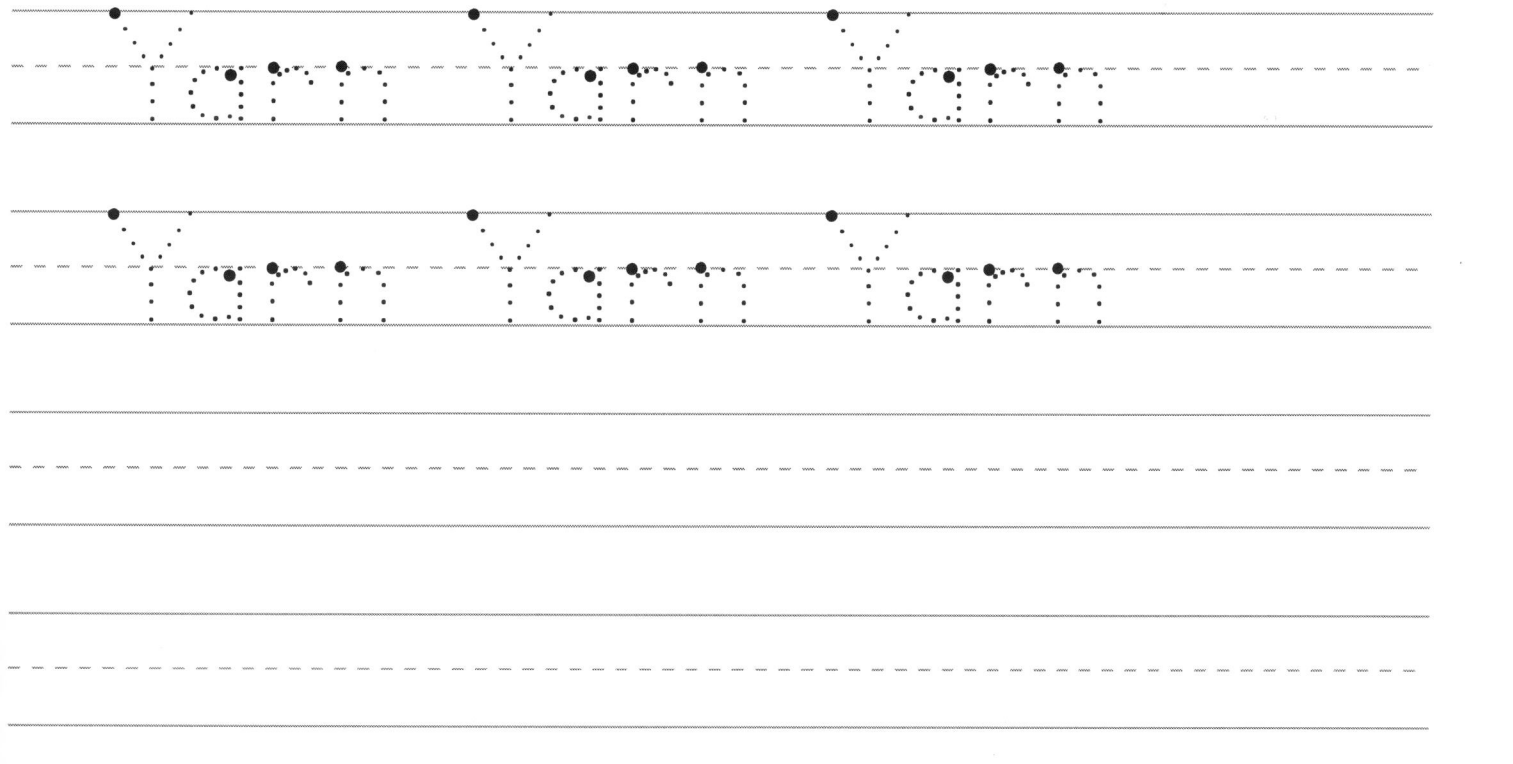

Yarn Yarn Yarn

Yarn Yarn Yarn

# Zebra

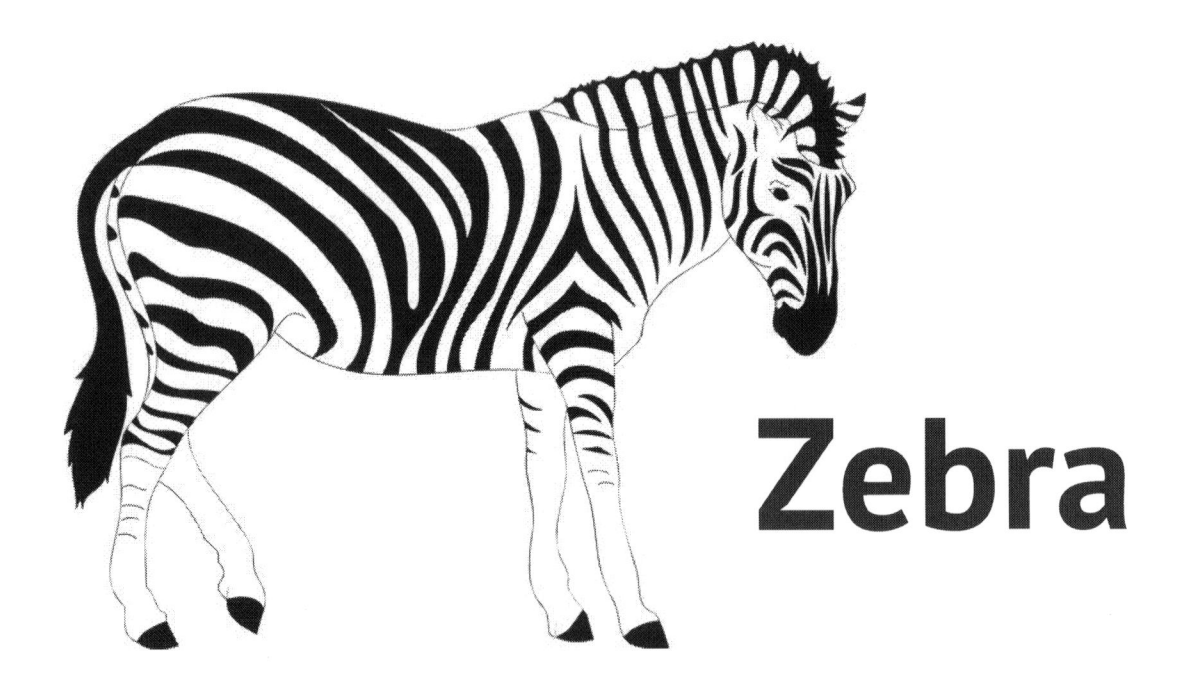

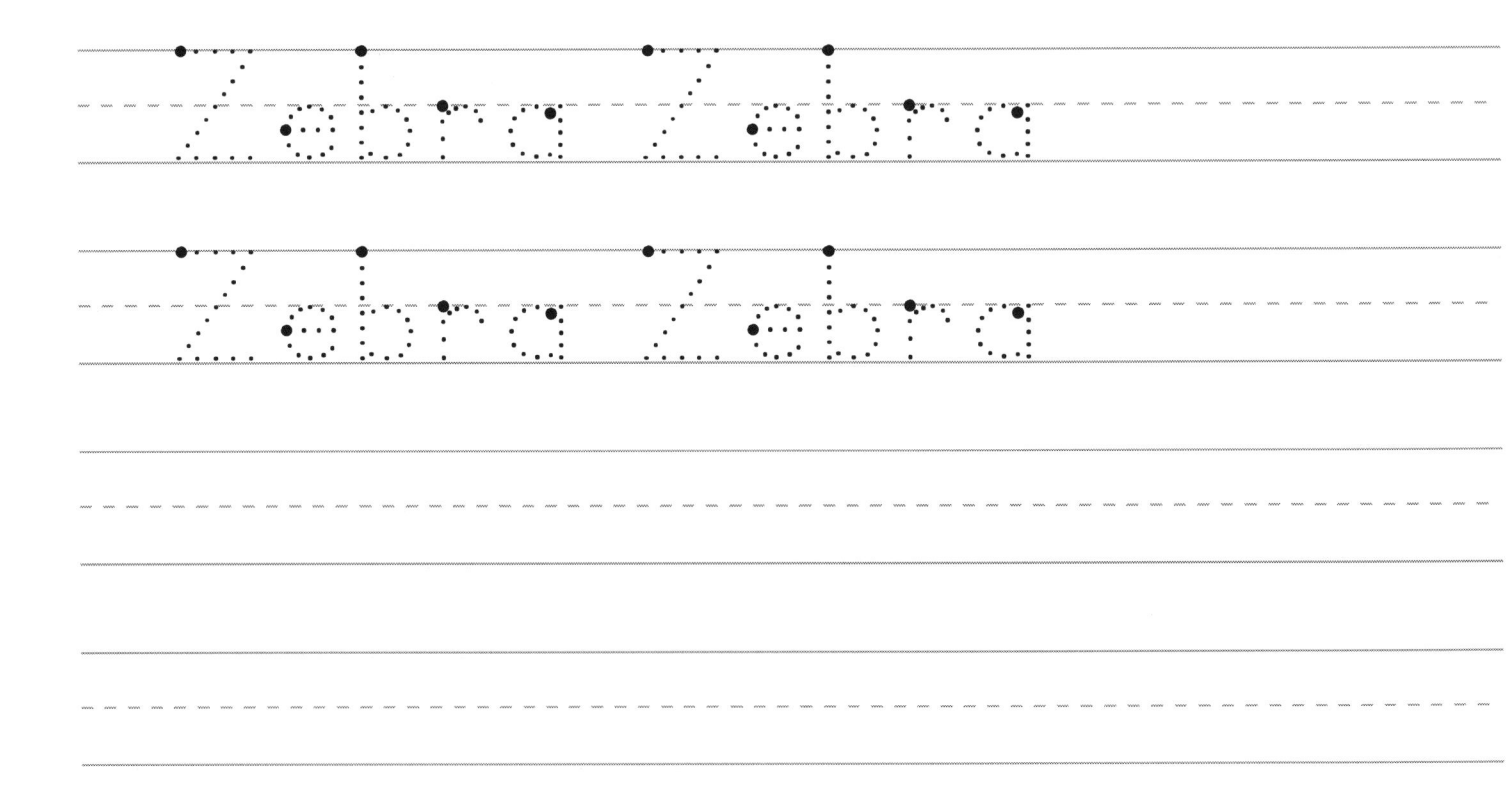

Zebra Zebra

Zebra Zebra

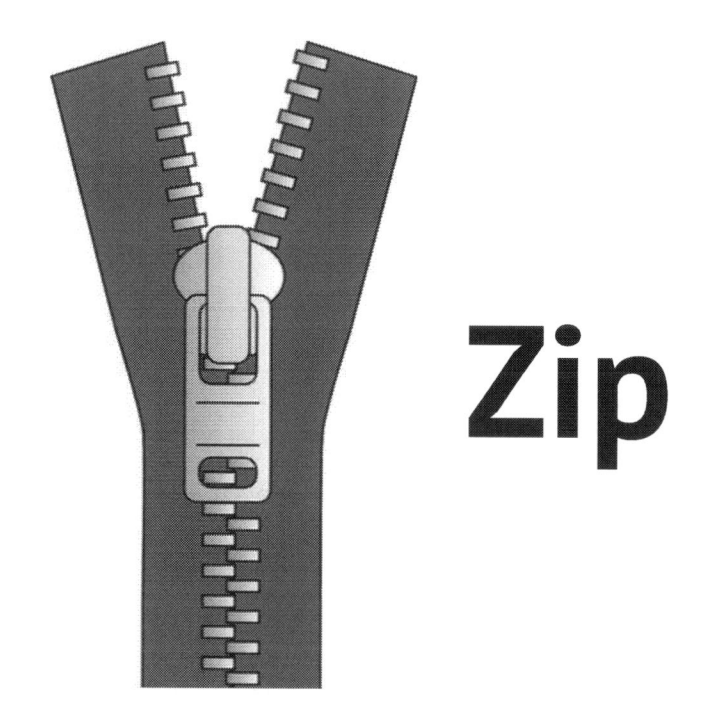

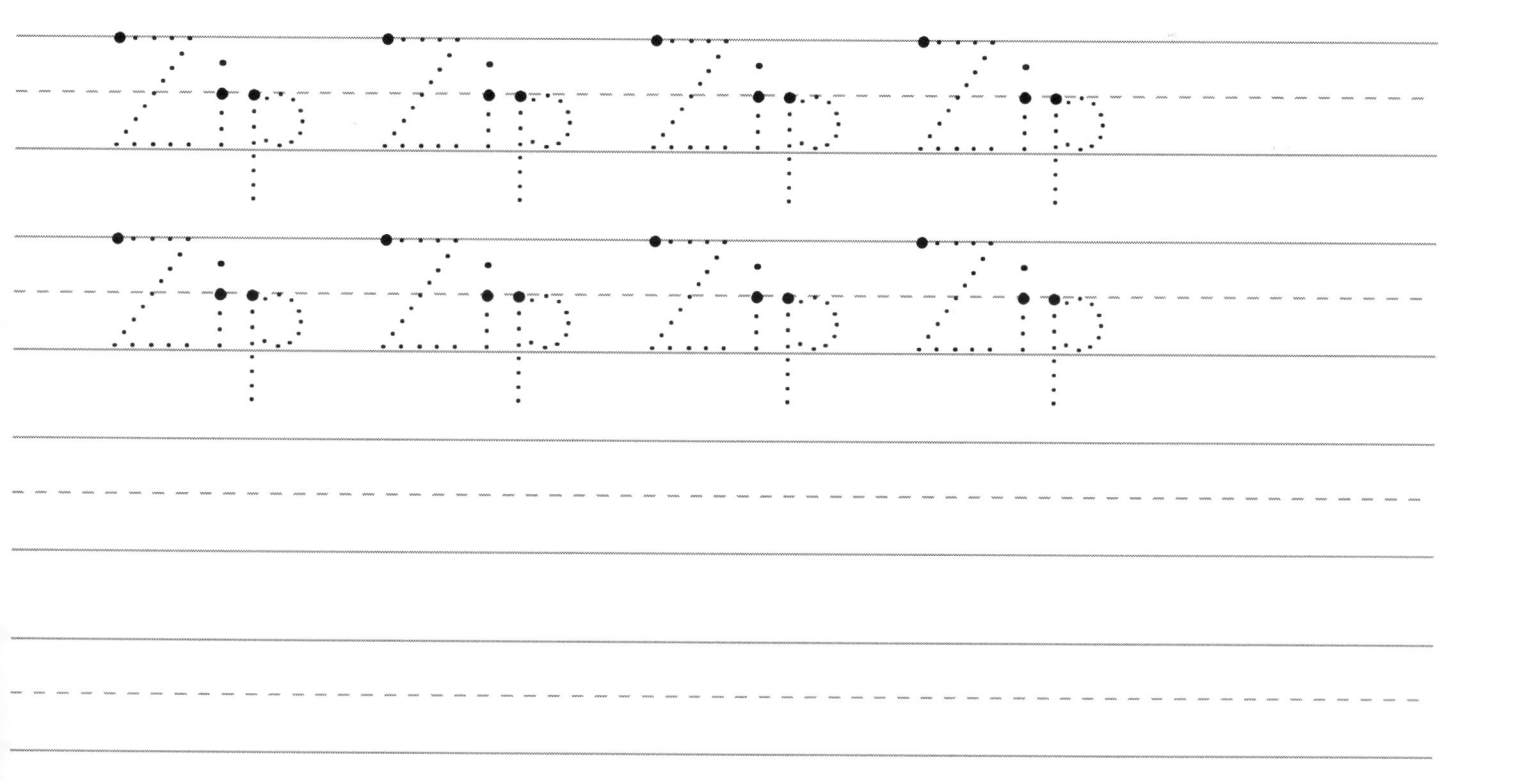

# Zip

Zip Zip Zip Zip

Zip Zip Zip Zip

Note:

Made in the USA
Middletown, DE
06 November 2019